KIDNER

CLASSIC COMMENTARIES

JEREMIAH

DEREK KIDNER

IVP Academic

An imprint of InterVarsity Press
Downers Grove, Illinois

InterVarsity Press, USA
P.O. Box 1400, Downers Grove, IL 60515-1426, USA
World Wide Web: www.ivpress.com
Email: email@ivpress.com

InterVarsity Press® is the book-publishing division of InterVarsity Christian Fellowship/USA®, a movement of students and faculty active on campus at hundreds of universities, colleges and schools of nursing in the United States of America, and a member movement of the International Fellowship of Evangelical Students. For information about local and regional activities, write Public Relations Dept., InterVarsity Christian Fellowship/USA, 6400 Schroeder Rd., P.O. Box 7895, Madison, WI 53707-7895, or visit the IVCF website at www.intervarsity.org.

Originally published as The Message of Jeremiah *in the Bible Speaks Today series.*

ISBN 978-1-7835-9143-5

Set in 11/12 pt Garamond
Typeset by Swanston Graphics Limited, Derby

Printed in the UK by 4edge Limited

 InterVarsity Press is committed to protecting the environment and to the responsible use of natural resources. As a member of Green Press Initiative we use recycled paper whenever possible. To learn more about the Green Press Initiative, visit www.greenpressinitiative.org.

Library of Congress Cataloging-in-Publication Data

Kidner, Derek
  The message of Jeremiah/Derek Kidner.
  p. cm.—(The Bible speaks today)
  Bibliography: p.
  ISBN 0-8308-1225-3 (U.S.: pbk.)
  1. Bible O.T. Jeremiah—Commentaries. I. Title. II. Series.
BS1524.3.K53 1987
224'.207—dc19

87-24492

| **P** | 18 | 17 | 16 | 15 | 14 | 13 | 12 | 11 | 10 | 9 | 8 | 7 | 6 | 5 | 4 | 3 | 2 | 1 |
| **Y** | 29 | 28 | 27 | 26 | 25 | 24 | 23 | 22 | 21 | 20 | 19 | 18 | 17 | 16 | 15 | 14 |

Publisher's preface

The Old Testament commentaries of Derek Kidner (1913–2008) have been a standard for a generation. His work has been model of conciseness, clarity and insight.

Kidner had a long career in both the church and the academy in England. After studying piano at the Royal College of Music, he prepared for the ministry at Cambridge University, where his musical interests found an outlet in performing in concerts of the Cambridge University Musical Society. He was then curate of St. Nicholas, Sevenoaks, south of London, before becoming Vicar of Felsted in Essex. After that he became a senior tutor at Oak Hill Theological College where he stayed for thirteen years. Kidner finished his career by serving as warden of Tyndale House in Cambridge from 1964 to 1978.

The year 1964 also marked the beginning of his writing career when his commentary on Proverbs was published. His ninth and final book, *The Message of Jeremiah,* was published in 1987. Those who read his books find in them the marks of both professor and pastor with his even-handed scholarship as well as his devotional insight. These qualities have made his commentaries in the Tyndale Old Testament Commentary series and The Bible Speaks Today series some of the most beloved and popular of recent decades.

As the commentaries in these two series have aged, the originating publisher, Inter-Varsity Press in England, began producing more up-to-date replacements which we at InterVarsity Press in the United States have been happy to publish as well. But knowing the honored place Kidner's work has had in the lives of so many students, teachers, lay people and pastors, we made the decision to keep his original volumes alive, but now as part of the Kidner Classic Commentaries. So we proudly and gladly offer these here for future generations to read, absorb and appreciate.

Author's preface

I am glad of the chance to express my thanks not only to those at the Inter-Varsity Press who saw this book safely into print, but above all to Mary, my long-suffering wife, who put up with a preoccupied husband during the slow writing of it.

But a preface also gives me room to put the subtitle, 'Against wind and tide', into its context. It comes, of course, from *The Pilgrim's Progress*, at the point where Christian overtakes Mr By-ends. That easygoing character admits his difference 'in two small points' from 'those of the stricter sort' – those who 'are for hazarding all for God at a clap'. 'First', he says, 'we never strive against wind and tide. Secondly, we are always most zealous when Religion goes in his silver slippers...' To this, Christian replies, 'If you will go with us, you must go against wind and tide; ...You must also own Religion in his rags, as well as when in his silver slippers; and stand by him, too, when bound in irons...

Such – initially under bitter protest, but with no turning back – was the hard pilgrimage that Jeremiah accepted, lending its own depth to his message. To study that life and message we can well be invited in John Bunyan's words:

> *Who would true valour see,*
> *Let him come hither.*
> *One here will constant be,*
> *Come wind, come weather.*

DEREK KIDNER

Contents

Publisher's preface   5

Author's preface   7

Chief abbreviations   10

Introduction: The life and times of Jeremiah   13

Prologue: The prophet's call (Jeremiah 1)   23

1 From Josiah to the first year of Nebuchadrezzar
   'If they do this when the wood is green . . .' (Jeremiah 2—20)   29

2 From Josiah's successors to the captivity
   '. . . what will happen when the wood is dry?'
   (Jeremiah 21—45)   83

3 Oracles concerning the nations (Jeremiah 46—51)   137

   Epilogue: Jerusalem and Babylon—A historical foonote
   (Jeremiah 52)   159

Appendices
   A Sin, judgment, repentance, grace and salvation in the
       preaching of Jeremiah   163
   B The chapters of the book in their chronological setting   173
   C A table of dates   177

Chief abbreviations

ANET	J. B. Pritchard (ed.), *Ancient Near Eastern Texts* (Princeton University Press, 3rd edition 1969).
AV	The Authorized (King James) Version of the Bible, 1611.
BDB	F. Brown, S. R. Driver and C. A. Briggs, *Hebrew–English Lexicon of the Old Testament* (Oxford University Press, 1907).
Bright	J. Bright, *Jeremiah* (*Anchor Bible*, Doubleday, 1965).
c.	*circa*, about.
ch(s).	chapter(s).
GNB	The Good News Bible (Today's English Version) (The Bible Society and Collins: NT 1966, 4th edition 1976; OT 1976).
Harrison	R. K. Harrison, *Jeremiah and Lamentations* (*Tyndale Old Testament Commentaries*, IVP, 1973).
Heb.	Hebrew.
IBD	J. D. Douglas (ed.), *Illustrated Bible Dictionary* (IVP, 1980).
JB	The Jerusalem Bible (Darton, Longman & Todd, 1966).
Keil	C. F. Keil, *Jeremiah and Lamentations*, 2 vols (*Biblical Commentary on the Old Testament by C. F. Keil and E. Delitzsch*, 1872: ET reprinted by Wm. B. Eerdmans, 1980).
K–B	L. Koehler and W. Baumgartner (eds), *Lexicon in Veteris Testamenti Libros* (E. J. Brill, 1958).
lit.	literally.
LXX	The Septuagint (pre-Christian Greek Version of the Old Testament).
mg.	margin.
McKane	*Jeremiah*, 1 (*International Critical Commentary, new series*, T. & T. Clark, 1986).
Moffatt	James Moffatt, *A New Translation of the Bible* (Hodder & Stoughton, 2nd edition 1935).
NBD	J. D. Douglas (ed.), *New Bible Dictionary* (IVP, 3rd edition 1982).

NEB	The New English Bible (The Bible Society and Oxford and Cambridge University Presses: NT 1961, 2nd edition 1970; OT 1970).
NIV	The New International Version of the Bible (International Bible Society and Hodder & Stoughton, 1973, 1978, 1984).
Phillips	J. B. Phillips, *The New Testament in Modern English* (Geoffrey Bles, 1960).
RSV	The Revised Standard Version of the Bible (Division of Christian Education of the National Council of the Churches in the USA: NT 1946, 2nd edition 1971, OT 1952).
RV	The Revised Version of the Bible (1881).
sc.	namely.
Skinner	J. Skinner, *Prophecy and Religion: Studies in the Life of Jeremiah* (Cambridge University Press, 1922).
Smith	G. A. Smith, *Jeremiah* (Hodder & Stoughton, 4th edition 1929).
Streane	A. W. Streane, *Jeremiah and Lamentations* (*Cambridge Bible for Schools and Colleges*, Cambridge University Press, 1899).
Syr.	Syriac version.
v(v).	verse(s).
Vg.	The Vulgate (Latin translation of the Bible by Jerome, fourth century AD).

Introduction
The life and times of Jeremiah

In the last decade of the longest, darkest reign in Judah's history, two boys were born who were to be God's gifts to a demoralized and damaged people. The reign was that of Manasseh, a half-century of deliberate reversion to the deities of Canaan and Assyria, to the black arts of magic and necromancy, to human sacrifice (even in the king's own family), and to such travesties of justice that, in the language of 2 Kings 21:16, 'he had filled Jerusalem from one end to another' with 'innocent blood'.

The two new lives in question were those of Josiah, born in 648 BC, and Jeremiah, perhaps his slightly younger contemporary. (At his call in 627 Jeremiah protested that he was 'only a youth'; and his subsequent ministry of over forty arduous years suggests that he was speaking literally.) As reforming king and outspoken prophet, these two were to give their country its finest opportunity of renewal and its last hope of surviving as the kingdom of David.

The previous century and its legacy

To set the scene, we should see this small kingdom as part of Syria-Palestine, that bone of contention between two great powers, Egypt to the south-west and Assyria to the north-east. For the last hundred years, from 745 onwards, a series of powerful Assyrian monarchs had brought this region firmly into their empire, exacting homage and yearly tribute from each petty state, on pain of swift revenge for defiance or default.

Israel, Judah's sister kingdom, had soon rebelled, only to have her northern and eastern tribes deported in 734/3. Finally, after a second revolt, her capital city was taken in 722/1 and her existence as a kingdom brought to an end.

So the tiny kingdom of Judah, herself a vassal of Assyria, had found herself sisterless, bounded on the north now by Assyrian provinces under foreign governors. Nothing daunted, however, her adventurous new king Hezekiah had soon swept away the religious emblems of Canaan and Assyria (the latter being part of the treaty-terms imposed on every vassal state) and was eventually in open rebellion, egged on as Israel had been, by Egypt. The cost was terrible. In 701 Sennacherib of Assyria had reduced the country almost to a desert:

> Your country lies desolate,
>   your cities are burned with fire ...;
> And the daughter of Zion is left
>   like a booth in a vineyard ...[1]

Although Jerusalem was miraculously spared in response to Hezekiah's and Isaiah's faith, the country's devastation that confronted Hezekiah's son Manasseh as he grew up evidently burnt its intended lesson into his mind. He broke with everything his father had stood for.

This, then, was the political dimension to the misdeeds of his long reign which were outlined in the opening paragraph above. Interestingly, his name 'Manasseh (Menasi), king of Judah', appears on a treaty-tablet drawn up in 672, whereby each vassal swore to treat the chief Assyrian god Asshur as his own god.[2] As we have seen, for Manasseh this was no reluctant blasphemy but part of the deliberate apostasy whereby he taught his people to 'do evil with both hands earnestly' (as Micah had said of an earlier generation: Mi. 7:3, AV). His eventual repentance[3] came too late to undo the damage. The early chapters of Jeremiah reveal a people still steeped in pagan worship and pagan morals, some fifteen years after Manasseh's death.

Yet the tide was about to turn.

---

[1] Is. 1:7a, 8a. Sennacherib records the capture of forty-six walled cities and 'countless small villages', and his eviction of '200,150 people'. See *ANET*, p. 288.

[2] D. J. Wiseman, *Illustrations from Biblical Archaeology* (IVP, 1958), p. 66. *Cf. ANET*, p. 291.

[3] 2 Ch. 33:10–17.

An all-out effort for reform

The boy-king Josiah had begun to seek the Lord in his teens, and at the age of twenty he began to purge his country of idolatry. One year later, in 627, Jeremiah began his long career as a prophet.

Meanwhile, abroad, Assyria was at last beginning to falter. For some years the edges of its vast empire had been under threat: with serious trouble in the east from Elam and the Medes, with steppe-dwellers raiding from the north, Arab tribes pouring into Edom and Moab from the Arabian desert, and disaffection in Syria and Palestine. Asshurbanipal was a strong enough king to suppress these movements, but his death in 627 (the year of Jeremiah's call) precipitated civil war over the succession, and, most ominously, saw the important city of Babylon breaking away to independence under a Chaldean named Nabopolassar. In 626 this man defeated the Assyrians outside Babylon and became its king. If his name is not a household word, his city and his son made up for this: Babylon as the centre of the neo-Babylonian empire which he founded, and Nebuchadrezzar[4] as its king from 605 to 562.

Josiah took advantage of this early turmoil to carry his reforms into the lost territory of Israel, right up to Naphtali in the far north,[5] before turning his attention to the temple in 622 and stumbling on the forgotten book of Mosaic law. For Jeremiah this discovery was to have momentous effects in at least three areas of his life.

First, after a national renewal of the covenant, based on the rediscovered book,[6] Jeremiah was sent on a preaching tour of 'the cities of Judah' and 'the streets of Jerusalem', to bring the challenge of it home to the nation.[7] This brought him the first threats against his life, and his first taste of rejection as a traitor to his upbringing. From his village and family such a reaction was only natural, for we may well imagine how the shock waves of the reform spread through priest-ridden Anathoth, where delight was followed by dismay with the arrival of the king's commissioners. Here, as in every place, the local altars were demolished, the heretical priests dismissed or even

---

[4] This spelling of his name, confined to Jeremiah and Ezekiel, is nearer to the Akkadian than the familiar form found in Daniel and elsewhere. But the latter is used also in Je. 27 – 29 (except at 29:21).

[5] 2 Ch. 34:6–7.

[6] 2 Ch. 34:29ff.

[7] Je. 11:1–8.

executed, and their legitimate colleagues transferred to serve in humbler capacities at Jerusalem.[8] For a son of the priesthood to throw himself into such a movement, no matter what divine authority it carried, was to put himself beyond the pale, 'a man of strife and contention to the whole land' (15:10). He escaped the murder plot but not the ostracism, nor again the divine compulsion that drove him on. Both are expressed in one of his poignant reflections on his lot:

> I did not sit in the company of merrymakers,
> > nor did I rejoice;
> I sat alone, because thy hand was upon me (15:17, cf. 20:7-9).

Secondly, the inward effect of this was to drive him into wrestling with God, in an agony of pleas and protests that we find scattered through chapters 11 – 20. Many are bitter and intensely personal:

> But I was like a gentle lamb
> > led to the slaughter.
> ... But thou, O Lord, knowest me; ...
> Pull them out like sheep for the slaughter ... (11:19; 12:3)

> Why is my pain unceasing,
> > my wound incurable ...?
> Wilt thou be to me like a deceitful brook,
> > like waters that fail? (15:18)

> I have become a laughingstock all the day;
> > every one mocks me ...
> If I say, 'I will not mention him,
> > or speak any more in his name,'
> there is in my heart as it were a burning fire
> > shut up in my bones,
> and I am weary with holding it in,
> > and I cannot (20:7b,9).

Other outpourings, of equal intensity, speak up for his whole people:

> O thou hope of Israel,
> > its saviour in time of trouble,

---

[8] See 2 Ki. 23:5–7, 19–20, for the idolatrous priests of Judah and Israel; and 2 Ki. 23:8–9 for the regular priests, in view of Dt. 12:13–14.

> why shouldst thou be like a stranger in the land, ...
>> like a mighty man who cannot save?
> Yet thou, O Lord, art in the midst of us,
>> and we are called by thy name;
>> leave us not (14:8–9).

In this crisis God replied to him in words which held him rigorously to his calling and assured him of survival:

> Let this people turn to you,
>> but you must not turn to them ...
> they will fight against you
>> but will not overcome you,
>> for I am with you ... (15:19b,20b, NIV).

So indeed it proved. The early ordeal, driving him to this desperate dialogue with God, was his baptism of fire. He emerged ready to stand his ground like a veteran, throughout the still fiercer sufferings of his final years.

But a third effect of his involvement in the reformation may have been even more far-reaching, for the experience revealed to him the inability of even the best of laws to reach the heart of a people for God. To take one blatant example, we are shown in 7:17ff. the popular worship of the queen of heaven in pre-reformation days; then in 44:15ff. we look back to its suppression by Josiah – only to find that more than thirty years later the reform still rankled. No attitudes had changed: only opportunities. The national covenant, like its original at mount Sinai, was broken almost as soon as made. No experience could have prepared a prophet better to hear God's promise of a new and better covenant[9] that would create a company of the converted and the era of the gospel.

Between the reforms of the 620s and the death of Josiah in 609 we know nothing of Jeremiah's career except that, in his own words, 'For twenty-three years, from the thirteenth year of Josiah ... to this day,[10] the word of the Lord has come to me, and I have spoken persistently to you, but you have not listened.' Yet, for all his unpopularity and the threats against his life (11:19; 12:6), the menace remained a war of nerves as long as Josiah still lived to protect him.

---

[9] Je. 31:31–34, *cf.* Mt. 26:28; 1 Cor. 11:25.

[10] He was speaking in 605, the fourth year of Josiah's son Jehoiakim (25:1ff.).

For Josiah himself there was increasing freedom to pursue his reforms and be a father to his people,[11] without hindrance from his nominal overlord Assyria, whose enemies were closing in, from Babylon in the south and Media on the east, until in 612 its capital city of Nineveh was taken. The Assyrian army retreated westward to Haran on the Euphrates, only to be pursued there and defeated by the Babylonians in 610.

Now Egypt took a hand, marching to the Euphrates in the hope of rescuing the Assyrians and of being rewarded with the gift of Syria and Palestine from their crumbling empire. This was the last thing that Josiah could want. Therefore in 609 he threw caution to the winds and intercepted the Egyptians at Megiddo, only to be defeated and killed in battle.

For Jeremiah and for Judah it was the end of an era. Although the Pharaoh failed to relieve the Assyrians, his army remained at the Euphrates, and he controlled Syria and Palestine for the next four years, deposing the new king of Judah and replacing him by another son of Josiah, the heavy-handed Jehoiakim. Then in 605 Nebuchadrezzar, the crown prince of Babylon, utterly routed the Egyptians at Carchemish on the Euphrates[12] and had the whole Near East at his feet.

It was in the next year[13] that Jeremiah had his collected prophecies read out to the people and to the king – only to have them burnt in the king's brazier.

Reaction, decline and fall

From this point on, Judah was committed to self-destruction. Paganism was again the order of the day, with all the old excesses and persecutions. For Jeremiah it brought a flogging and the pillory (20:2), and a close brush with death (26:10ff.). For a fellow prophet, Uriah, and for other inconvenient people there was no mercy.[14] Finally Jehoiakim, not content with breaking the divine covenant, broke faith with his new master, Nebuchadrezzar,[15] with the inevitable result. In December 598 Jehoiakim was deposed and put

[11] *Cf.* 22:15b–16.
[12] The rout is vividly portrayed in Je. 46:2–12.
[13] 36:9ff.
[14] 26:20–23; 22:17.
[15] 2 Ki. 24:1.

in fetters, to be deported to Babylon, but died at the outset of the journey. His successor, Jeconiah, barricaded Jerusalem against the Babylonian army, but surrendered after some three months, to be taken into exile along with the temple treasures and the cream of his citizens, on 16 March 597 BC.

After administering such a lesson it seemed safe to Nebuchadrezzar to appoint a royal nonentity as puppet-king, suitably sworn to loyalty. But Zedekiah was everybody's puppet, and was soon entertaining a delegation from nearby states, evidently come to talk rebellion.[16]

It was to be Jeremiah's greatest and most testing decade. God's will was now quite clear to him, but at every point it would seem madness to his generation. He startled the conspirators by appearing among them wearing an ox-yoke and demanding submission to Nebuchadrezzar. He followed this by writing to the captives, preparing them for a seventy-year exile and calling for a peaceable attitude to Babylon (29:7,10). It contradicted all that their firebrand prophets were telling them. Already it was a dangerous line to take, bringing him new threats of 'the stocks and collar' (29:24–29). But it was as nothing to the stand he had to adopt when Zedekiah broke his oath of fealty and brought an avenging Babylon to the gates. This, said Jeremiah, was from God, and it was judgment. There was nothing for it but acceptance, and if the king would not save the city by surrender (38:17), this was no reason why citizens should stay and perish there (38:2).

By any human reckoning this was treason, and Jeremiah tasted the rigours of a private dungeon, a military prison and, until his rescue, a miry pit that threatened to engulf him as he weakened. Throughout the siege he was tantalized by the king's tentative enquiries[17] and secret interviews,[18] all of which came to nothing through Zedekiah's irresolution.

Not treason, however, but sober faith was Jeremiah's motivation. While others dreamt of some last-minute deliverance like that of Hezekiah's day,[19] he held to what had been revealed: the twin certainties of captivity and return – even committing himself to the

---

[16] 27:3 (for the date, see 28:1).
[17] 21:1ff.; 37:3ff.
[18] 37:16ff.; 38:14.
[19] Is. 37:36–37, cf. Je. 21:2.

latter at the height of the siege by redeeming some family property in territory overrun by the enemy.[20] As for lack of proper patriotism: when the city fell in 587 and the victors offered him comfortable conditions in Babylon (40:4), he showed where his loyalties lay by electing to stay in his homeland with the poorest of the people and their new governor, Gedaliah, at Mizpah. In sad contrast, the king had fled with his army as soon as the city wall was breached, but was overtaken, blinded and deported to Babylon. As for Jerusalem, the policy of no surrender only succeeded in marking it out for a particularly thorough work of demolition,[21] making sure that it would give no further trouble.

The prophet's last years

Meanwhile for Jeremiah at Mizpah there was but the briefest respite. In the autumn of possibly the same year (41:1) Gedaliah was assassinated by a royal pretender named Ishmael, who had the backing of the king of Ammon. The coup was a failure, but the loyalists who thwarted it became aware that Babylon's reprisals for the death of its representative could well be crippling and indiscriminate. So in panic they decided on a massed migration to Egypt – but took the precaution of consulting Jeremiah before embarking on the journey. Characteristically Jeremiah waited patiently for a word from God; but when it came it was a clear instruction to call off the project, on pain of every kind of judgment (42:7ff.).

This made no impression. Jeremiah, to his hearers, was being merely his usual opinionated self, egged on doubtless by his too-confidential secretary Baruch (43:2–3). With one consent the whole company set out for Egypt, taking Jeremiah and Baruch with them. Our last glimpse of the prophet and his abductors is of a confrontation in which his charge of apostasy is thrown back at him with the countercharge that his kind of religion, flouting the age-old cults, had been the source of all their troubles.[22]

With his rejoinder that posterity would 'know whose word [would] stand, mine or theirs' (44:28), the record of Jeremiah's life

---

[20] 32:6–14, 24–25.
[21] 52:12ff.
[22] 44:1–14, 15–19.

breaks off, leaving simply his prophecies to speak for themselves. It is what he himself surely would have wished.

As a brief epilogue, we may remember that less than half a century later the first of the Babylonian exiles – but not the self-exiled in Egypt – would arrive home in their thousands, in living confirmation of the promises that matched the warnings of this prophet.[23] But we may also remember certain characters who would not live to see that day, but whose distinction was that they had stood by Jeremiah in his darkest years. Among the highest officials there were men enough to defend his 'Shiloh' sermon and save him from death, early in the reign of Jehoiakim (26:10ff.). Members of one family in particular, that of Shaphan, steadily took the lead in befriending him: Ahikam on this occasion (26:24), Gemariah and Micaiah his son at the reading of the prophecies (36:10, 11, 25), and finally the magnanimous Gedaliah, who took him under his wing at Mizpah (40:5–6). These were men of influence who had much to lose. Another, more precariously placed, being a foreigner, risked everything to save him from the miry pit (38:6–13; 39:15–18). This was Ebed-melech the Ethiopian, whose imaginative care and courage made his act of rescue unforgettable.

But we owe most of all to Baruch, who not only wrote out and read out the scroll of prophecies (36:4ff.) but almost certainly supplied the narrative framework of the book. What this cost him in toil and fear and in the sacrifice of his bright prospects, can be read in the short chapter 45. He responded well to the sternness of 45:5: 'And do you seek great things for yourself? Seek them not ...' – for the things he sought instead were 'great' in the sense that mattered, stored up not for himself but for every reader of what he preserved, from that day to this.

[23] *E.g.*, 29:10ff., *cf.* Ezr. 1:1 – 2:70.

PROLOGUE: Jeremiah 1
The prophet's call

The scene is set   1:1–3

There is more than meets the eye in this matter-of-fact announcement. For a start, we can notice the texture that it claims for the contents of the book, as at once human (*the words of Jeremiah*) and divine (*the word of the Lord*). God had shaped this highly individual personality not only to speak his message but to embody it, as a composer might entrust his most poignant passages to – shall we say – the cor anglais, or to an instrument of his own inventing; or as a painter might choose one medium rather than another to match and express his subject.

Then there are the notes of time and place. The time span tells its own story of endurance, in the prophet's forty years or more of preaching (627–587 BC and beyond); but there was more to it than length. It covered one of those tempestuous periods when the world at large goes into convulsion: in this case with Assyria's empire falling apart, and Egypt fighting in vain to keep Babylon from picking up the pieces – among which, ominously, was little Judah.[1] At home, too, the three kings named here, Josiah the reformer, Jehoiakim the tyrant and Zedekiah the weathercock, touched three

---

[1] See the Introduction for a historical outline of the times.

extremes of royal character[2] that created changes in the spiritual climate which were fully as violent as those of the political scene.

Even Jeremiah's home town of Anathoth (1:1) had its part to play in his career. As a settlement of priestly families (*cf.* 1 Ki. 2:26–27), whose status was suddenly threatened by Josiah's reformation, it was to give the prophet his first sharp taste of persecution.[3] Topographically, too, it may have had a share in his development, as George Adam Smith has persuasively suggested:

> It is the last village eastward, and from its site the land falls away in broken, barren hills to the north end of the Dead Sea. The vision of that desert maze was burnt into the prophet's mind, and he contrasted it with the clear, ordered Word of God. *O generation, see ye the word of the Lord: Have I been a wilderness unto Israel, a land of darkness?*[4] He had lived in face of the scorching desert air – *A dry wind of the high places in the wilderness toward the daughter of my people, not to fan, nor to cleanse.*[5] And in face of the chaotic prospect, he described judgment in these terms: *I beheld, ... and, lo, the fruitful place was a wilderness ... at the presence of the Lord, by his fierce anger.*[6]

Such were the times, the powers, the culture, to which this man was called to bring the word of God.

The call   1:4–19

If the first words of the book introduced us to its forty years of troubled history, God's opening words to Jeremiah himself unveiled a larger setting and a longer story.

---

[2] See ch. 22 for assessments of Jehoiakim (13–19) and Josiah (15b–16); also chs. 36 and 37 – 38 for characteristic glimpses of Jehoiakim and Zedekiah in action.

[3] 11:19–23; 12:6.

[4] 2:31, AV.

[5] 4:11, AV.

[6] 4:23, 26, AV. G. A. Smith, *The Historical Geography of the Holy Land* (Hodder & Stoughton,[13] 1907), pp. 315–316.

No casual choice   1:4–5

To be told, *Before I formed you in the womb I knew you*, was to be given at once a new centre of gravity, away from his sole self and from the confines of the immediate scene, back to the Creator himself and to the master-plan. The very expression, *I formed you*, brought its own hint of the potter's care and skill (one day to be expounded further and applied more widely at the potter's house, in ch. 18) – lest it should ever seem to Jeremiah that his sensitive and vulnerable nature was a cruel accident. He was handmade for his task.

Already – given the title, 'The Bible Speaks Today' – we have to ask how much of this can fairly be applied to others besides Jeremiah. The rest of the verse will be specific to him, but the New Testament speaks to every Christian in terms that are comparable to those that we have seen: 'For those whom he foreknew he also predestined to be conformed to the image of his Son ...' (Rom. 8:29). These are terms which are meant to reassure and reorientate us, no less than those that Jeremiah heard: not invitations to puzzle out the relation of time to eternity, or of human choices to divine. The warmth of God's saying to us as to Jeremiah, in effect, 'I have *always* known you, and my hands have formed and fashioned you',[7] is too magnificent to dissipate in speculation. An answering warmth of gratitude, in awed acceptance, is the only fit response.

Then, with a second *Before* ..., to underline this deliberate choice, the words, *I knew*, are amplified with *I consecrated* and *I appointed*, relating Jeremiah first to his Lord and then to his world. Long before this, God had said these two things about the temple servants, explaining their consecration and their commission in strong, simple terms: 'I have *taken* them for myself ... and I have *given* [them] as a gift to Aaron and his sons ...'[8] The same word, 'given', is used of Jeremiah here, rightly translated *appointed* (for Hebrew closely connects the acts of giving, placing and appointing).[9] It completed God's act of taking or consecrating his servant, for he takes in order to give, in the many senses of that word. This, incidentally, corrects any tendency to think of sanctity too introspectively; and it is borne out by our Lord's description of

---

[7] *Cf.* Ps. 119:73.
[8] Nu. 8:16c, 19.
[9] *Cf.* Eph. 4:11.

himself as 'consecrated and sent' (Jn. 10:36), and by his words, *'for their sake* I consecrate myself ' (Jn. 17:19).

No eager prophet 1:6

Jeremiah's shrinking from the call had at least one asset to it: in years to come he could never accuse himself of having taken on his role out of self-importance or for the subtle pleasure of creating consternation.

> I have not pressed thee to send evil,
>   nor have I desired the day of disaster (17:16).

His dismay at his call, and his later struggles to keep silent (20:9), gave their own witness to the divine, not human, compulsion he was under. And unlike Moses, whose protestations of inadequacy rang a little hollow,[10] Jeremiah really was young, it seems, and inexperienced.

The real point 1:7–8

God's reply has something for others besides Jeremiah, for it is typical of his approach to human misgivings. What Jeremiah had said about himself might well be true (God did not deny it) but it was not the point. The proper question was not, 'Who am I to do this?' but 'What are my instructions? Where am I posted? And will God be with me?' God's reply (7–8) put the whole matter on the right footing and related it to its true centre: the master, not the servant.

A touch and two signs 1:9–16

The touch of God, ever creative, together with the words that clarified it, put beyond doubt the givenness of the message and the mandate of the messenger. It would not spare Jeremiah the heart-searching and mental wrestling he was to go through, but it put his commission beyond all doubt.

We could wish, perhaps, that we too were given something as tangible as this, along with God's spoken promises. But we are. He,

---

[10] Ex. 4:10ff., *cf.* Acts 7:22.

like a friend who puts an encouraging and affectionate hand on one's shoulder, has added touch to speech. 'You were washed ...'; 'Take, eat ..., drink ...'[11] His are no arm's-length dealings; and when sight and hearing fail us he still keeps open his pre-arranged signals for us.

Jeremiah's commission set the pattern of his calling, with its four verbs of demolition and its two of renewal (*to build and to plant*, 10). He would stand on the brink of the Exile, that great divide of Israel's history, and would call the nations to accept the yoke of Babylon (chs 27 – 29). But in God's name, too, he would announce the shortness of the years allotted to that empire,[12] and the mercy in store for Israel and for the teachable among the nations.[13]

After the overwhelming touch of God, the two signs – a sprig of almond, and a cooking pot on an outdoor fire – were as unremarkable as Amos's 'basket of summer fruit' or the barren fig tree in the gospel.[14] But they crystallized the message and fixed it sharply in the mind. What was more, the first of them, the almond sprig, would repeat its message year after year, if Jeremiah would have eyes to see it.

The almond (1:11–12), by its name, 'wakeful',[15] proclaims itself the earliest to greet the spring. So too, when all seems dormant, God is wakeful, ready for his moment to fulfil his word. In the companion picture, that word will be of judgment; but here is hope, a living token of hidden promise and of God's silent, creative energy.

The seething cauldron (13–16), tilting dangerously as the fire settled, made a terribly appropriate picture of the menace from the north (the old invasion route of Assyria, soon to be that of Babylon); and it remains as apt as ever to the human scene where, from one quarter after another, human aggressiveness lets loose a scalding stream of havoc. Nothing could be less like the quiet and creative promise of the previous picture, yet God would not only tolerate it: he would summon it (*calling all the tribes of the kingdoms of the north*, 15) to engulf his land. To be 'God's own people' – even when this was fact, not fantasy – carried no diplomatic immunity, rather the

---

[11] 1 Cor. 6:11; Mt. 26:26–27.
[12] 25:11–14; 27:7; 29:10–14.
[13] *Cf.* 12:14–17; 46:26, *etc.*
[14] Am. 8:1–2; Mk. 11:12–14.
[15] Heb. *šāqēḏ* from the same root as the word 'watching' (*šōqēḏ*) in v. 12.

reverse, as Amos had pointed out long before.[16] But the idea dies hard!

A time to speak out 1:17–19

With the words, *But you* (17), the tone is suddenly bracing (how well we know that change from the general to the personal!), for Jeremiah is not simply being let into a secret. There is sharp wisdom in the call to keep nothing back, but to *say ... everything that I command you* – for in the first place a spokesman must get it clear *whose* mind he is there to express, and in the second place he must put away timidity, for in this realm to bend over backwards is to fall. In fact God goes further with the warning, *lest I dismay you before them.* He is not committed to keeping 'Mr Anything' or 'Mr Two-Tongues' out of trouble (to borrow two of Bunyan's characters, commended by Mr By-Ends).

But the stern call came with – as ever – an equally strong promise: in this case a triple guarantee of survival. To this thin-skinned young man, his description in terms of battlements and heavy metal might have seemed a wild exaggeration, but in fact it proved an understatement. He would hold out against all comers for over forty years, outdoing any fortress under siege; and his strength would be not the inert solidity of iron, but the courage of a frail man's hard-won convictions.

The climax of God's charge put frankly the two sides of what awaited him: *They will fight against you; but ... I am with you* – for God does not cut the knot. For Jeremiah or for us, his way in general is not to stop the fight but to stand by the fighter. He is forming a company of veterans, 'called and chosen and faithful',[17] of whom he can say that he 'is not ashamed to be called their God'.[18]

---

[16] Am. 3:2.
[17] Rev. 17:14.
[18] Heb. 11:16.

PART ONE: Jeremiah 2 – 20

From Josiah to the first year of Nebuchadrezzar

'If they do this when the wood is green ...'

Jeremiah started to prophesy in the thirteenth year of King Josiah (627 BC), which was one year after the beginning of that king's reformation movement (2 Ch. 34:3). Four years after Josiah's death (the fourth year of Jehoiakim and the first of Nebuchadrezzar (*cf.* 25:1), *i.e.* 605), Jeremiah was commanded to write all his prophecies on a scroll and have them read out to the nation (ch. 36). That scroll was destroyed but rewritten, and this collecting of his output of the first twenty-three years (*cf.* 25:3) marks the turning-point in his ministry. Such a point seems to be reached by chapter 20, after which most of the chapters up to chapter 45 carry dates from 605 onwards, which we treat as Part Two. But the scarcity of dates in Part One, and the fact that subject-matter counts for more than chronology in the arrangement of the book, makes this division no more than a rough guide. What he was given to say, rather than when it was said, must be our great concern.

The betrayal of love   2:1–37

The word of the Lord came (but more literally it 'became') to a mind stored with revealed history and sensitized by the appeals of earlier prophets, especially (it seems) by Hosea, the prophet of God's family-love.

The fickle bride   2:1–13

There is the freshness of spring in the Lord's first words to Israel, recapturing the ardour of young love – that readiness of the beloved to go anywhere, put up with anything, so long as it could be shared with her partner; and on his side the fierce protectiveness that would brook no rival, no slight on her honour.[1] To begin on such a note was the way to awaken any spark of longing or compunction that might still lie dormant in the hearers (for affection can disarm us where a scolding only rankles). But it also set the keynote of the opening chapters, which are tragically dominated by the later history of this divine–human marriage. Whatever else was wrong with Israel – and there was no lack of it – the violated marriage was fundamental.

So in this chapter the Lord concentrates on the sheer perversity of her unfaithfulness, before going on in 3:1 – 4:4 to raise the question whether the marriage is now beyond repair.

To glance first at the overall shape of this impassioned chapter, we find its reproaches aimed alternately at the primary and at the secondary sins of Israel – that is, at her embracing of heathen gods (5–13, 20–32) and at her flirtation with heathen empires (14–19, 33–37). Each of these themes is presented with the utmost intensity.

First, then, the primary sin: that of the quitter, the unfaithful partner. It is dealt with in plain terms first of all (5–13), but then illustrated in a flurry of word-pictures in verses 20–32, portraying

---

[1] Witness the dire penalties against Amalek (Dt. 25:17–19) and Moab (Dt. 23:3–6) for tampering with God's people on the march. The 'first-fruits' metaphor is drawn from the law that claimed these for God alone (*e.g.*, Lv. 19:23–24, *cf.* Ho. 9:10; Am. 6:1). C. F. Keil points out that in the brief time of espousals (a more accurate translation than 'as a bride'), *i.e.*, from the Passover to the covenant at Sinai, Israel cast no eyes towards other gods, for all her failures of faith and patience.

Israel in one unflattering guise after another, from human down to animal.

At once we meet that mixture of the perverse, the frivolous and the ungrateful which is typical of all sin. Perversity is immediately shown up by the question, *What wrong did your fathers find in me that they went far from me?* (5) – to which a candid answer might have been, 'Too little wrong! Give us a god with our own failings!' Or else, 'We never asked that kind of question: all we wanted was a change' – for that is the frivolous attitude implied in going after *worthlessness* (5b), exchanging the real for the unreal, the eternal for the ephemeral.[2] As for ingratitude, it is the egoist's defence against embarrassing self-knowledge – for to have needed a benefactor, or worse still, a rescuer, is something best forgotten. So to Israel, the old story of their exodus, their miraculous journey and their promised land (5–7), had lost all its appeal: for who wants to be perpetually reminded (they might have said) of what he owes? The fact that, like their fathers, 'they soon forgot' (Ps. 106:13), owed more to pride than to a poor memory.

Just how deep and wide this alienation went is spelt out in verse 8, with its priests whose routines revolved round themselves, with its scholars who knew everything but the Lord, with its rulers who ignored the rules, and – most blatantly of all – with its prophets to whose broad minds Yahweh and Baal were all one. We might almost be reading of our own day.

What also strikes a chord with us is the paradox of the next verses (9–13), summed up in verse 11:

> *Has a nation changed its gods,*
> *even though they are no gods?*
> *But my people have changed their glory*
> *for that which does not profit*

– for we have the spectacle, in our own time, of whole nations blindly loyal to their religions and ideologies, while those that have known the true God grow weary, like Israel, of even his first commandment. If this is perfidy it is also lunacy. The little parable of verse 13 on exchanging *living waters* for *broken cisterns* says it all; and to those who knew the latter from experience it would have spoken volumes. To quote one observer from the last century,

---

[2] 'Worthlessness' here is *hebel*, the 'vanity' of Ec. 1:2, *etc.*

> The best cisterns, even those in solid rock, are strangely liable to crack ..., and if by constant care they are made to hold, yet the water collected from clay roofs or from marly soil has the colour of weak soapsuds, the taste of the earth or the stable, is full of worms, and in the hour of greatest need it utterly fails.[3]

To point the contrast still more sharply, a later passage will dwell on the majestic flow of living waters, unfailing, endlessly refreshing – and rejected:

> Does the snow of Lebanon
> ever vanish from its rocky slopes?
> Do its cool waters from distant sources
> ever cease to flow?
> Yet my people have forgotten me ... (Je. 18:14–15a, NIV).

The easy prey 2:14–19

Turning now to the way in which the same treachery has coloured their politics, we are shown Israel running from one great power to another, with not a thought of loyalty to God or man. It is folly as well as sin – for they were never meant to be at the beck and call of an overlord. They are sons, not slaves (14a). Moreover they are playing with predators (see what ravages they have made already! 15ff.); they have left their true protector, who *led [them] in the way* (17), and they have made that special rod for their own back which is the traitor's lot (19):

> *Your wickedness will chasten you*
> *and your apostasy will reprove you.*
> *Know and see that it is evil and bitter*
> *for you to forsake the Lord your God.*

The hard case 2:20–32

We return here to the basic theme of Israel as the truant wife, pictured now in one unflattering guise after another: from avid prostitute to unmanageable child, from wild vine to wild ass, each with the instant impact and penetration of a cartoonist's line-drawing.

[3] W. H. Thomson, *The Land and the Book* (Harper, 1886), p. 287, quoted in Streane, p. 17.

The first of these (20) was all too apt, with its picture of a restless wife to whom the bonds and burdens of true love were slavery, and the lure of the forbidden irresistible. And there was more than metaphor in the outspoken language here,[4] since Baal-worship was licentious as well as false: preoccupied with fertility, which it attributed to the copulations not only of gods and goddesses but of male and female cult-prostitutes with worshippers at the shrines.

Does the Bible here speak only to the past? True, the Canaanite ideology is no longer with us; yet polytheism and pantheism are far from dead, and any religion that has room for promiscuous gods is liable to imitate them. Further, the 'sexual revolution' introduced in the 1960s is not only permissive: it has its own propaganda to create a view of sex as virtually life's chief concern and most authoritative voice – certainly one that can override the voice of God. Nor is this only the view of secularists. Progressive churchmen can be found to echo it.[5]

The main thrust, nevertheless, of Jeremiah's cry of 'harlot!' is aimed at the heart of the matter: not the physical but the spiritual promiscuity of this runaway bride of Yahweh. In what follows, we have God's angle on the liberties we are apt to take with him, on which we may even pride ourselves. To him, as these swift vignettes reveal, our daring thoughts and ways are anything but impressive. A glance at each metaphor is enough:

> degenerate vine (21) – back to nature, back to uselessness;
> vain ablutions (22–23a) – as if there were a home-remedy for guilt;
> restive colt (23b, 36) – leading everyone a dance;
> wild ass on heat (24–25) – doubly unbiddable: untamed and infatuated;
> thief caught out (26) – not as clever as he thought;
> problem family (30) – tearing itself apart;
> nonchalant bride (32) – but no! The comparison collapses. No jewel, no wedding dress, could ever mean as little to its owner as God does to his own!

---

[4] The verb translated 'bowed down' (RSV) or 'lay down' (NIV) is well rendered 'sprawled' (NEB).

[5] For an example in print, cf. the comment of the Rev. H. A. Williams on a story of psychological release through the attentions of a prostitute: 'And where there is healing, there is Christ, whatever the church may say about fornication. And the appropriate response is – Glory to God in the Highest.' A. R. Vidler (ed.), *Soundings* (CUP, 1963), p. 82.

The impenitent   2:33–37

The first verse of the section (33) takes up again the unlovely portrait of the harlot with which verses 20–32 opened. There (20b) she was the embodiment of lust; here, of sophistication and guile – for it was as true then as now, that the pagan has nothing to teach the hardened apostate,[6] nor the outright unbeliever the religious double-thinker. 'How skilled you are …!' (33, NIV).

Finally the alternating emphasis of the chapter comes back to the manward outcome of the Godward sin. With God dethroned, nothing is unthinkable: not even murder – here quite literally, since the regime of king Manasseh (in whose reign Jeremiah was born) had 'filled Jerusalem from one end to another' with 'innocent blood' (2 Ki. 21:16), which included human sacrifice.[7] This blood was still clinging to them (34a), for they had never taken it to heart and sought forgiveness.[8] To the new generation it was something to shrug off.

But Scripture often stresses the solidarity of one generation with another, endorsing our sense of pride or shame over our collective past. It is easily abused, whether by the bravado of verse 35, when we defend the indefensible and rewrite history in our favour; or when we keep alive old enmities, as Edom did, who 'kept his wrath for ever' (Am. 1:11); or when we blame on the past all the ills of the present (Ezk. 18:2, *cf.* Je. 31:29). A healthier attitude is seen in the great confessions of Ezra 9, Nehemiah 9 and Daniel 9, and in sharing God's overriding concern with the present and the future, which he expounded at the potter's house in Jeremiah 18:1–11.

Finally, if guilt sat lightly upon this people, no less so did their promises – for the opportunist hates all talk of obligation. He must not be pinned down. But his artful moves are seen here through the eyes of God as anything but statesmanlike. They are a mere scurrying to and fro (36),[9] doomed to the humiliation they deserve. A century before this, Hosea had warned the northern kingdom

---

[6] *Cf.* 2 Ki. 21:9 '… and Manasseh seduced them to do more evil than the nations had done whom the Lord destroyed before the people of Israel'.

[7] 2 Ki. 21:6, to which we may add the question, What of our own society's murders of convenience? What is more innocent than an embryo?

[8] The words, 'you did not find them breaking in' (34), refer to the law of Ex. 22:2, excusing the killing of a thief caught forcing an entrance at night. No vestige of such an excuse could apply to Judah's guilt.

[9] 'Gad about' RSV is too light-hearted for this word, which tends to speak of impermanence rather than frivolity.

against these frantic overtures to east and west; and now in Jeremiah's lifetime Judah would play the same dangerous games with them, only to lose two kings to Egypt[10] and a final two to Assyria's successor, Babylon.[11]

Cheap repentance? 3:1 – 4:4

There is a problem with free forgiveness. If you can always wipe the slate clean, how much does it matter what you write on it next? It is a problem for both parties – not only for the one in the wrong, who may feel that he can get away with more and more, but also for the one who forgives, who has to wonder what his forbearance may be doing to the other person. Here God sets about shaking his people out of their complacency.

A chilling question 3:1–5

God still keeps to the analogy of the broken marriage, but now administers a shock from the law-books – perhaps from the very scroll that was so dramatically discovered at about this time (for v. 1 refers to Dt. 24:1–4). This law, which forbade a divorced couple to reunite, was aimed against what would amount to virtually *lending* one's partner to another – for if an authoritarian husband could dismiss his wife and have her back when the next man had finished with her, it would degrade not only her but marriage itself and the society that accepted such a practice.

But there was more than a principle to bar the way home. *This* wife, this kingdom of Judah, was no passive shuttlecock between one husband and another, but brazenly promiscuous, installing her lovers, her gods and goddesses, on every hilltop (2), to charm the rain out of the sky and the corn out of the earth in the time-honoured way of Canaan (see the comment on 2:20). What

[10] 2 Ki. 23:29, 31–34.
[11] 2 Ki. 24:15; 25:7. For Egypt's ineffective backing for the final rebellion, see Ezk. 17:15, 17; Je. 37:7.

made it insufferable was the pious talk that went with it, appealing to Yahweh's fatherhood, friendship and forbearance (4–5): talk which only added hypocrisy to infidelity:

> *Behold, you have spoken,*
>   *but you have done all the evil that you could* (5).

A startling comparison   3:6–11

God's third line of attack (3:6–25) must have stung Judah to the quick. Instead of pointing to her notorious sister Israel as an awful warning and as the black sheep of the family, he gives that distinction to the present company. Israel had turned her back on God and paid the penalty – but Judah had seen it all and followed suit, sinning with her eyes open. To make it worse, she had put on a sanctimonious show of repentance and reform. Defection was one thing; make-believe was quite another. *Judah did not return to me with her whole heart, but in pretence, says the Lord ... Faithless Israel has shown herself less guilty than false Judah* (10–11).[12]

A humbling invitation   3:12–18

Now, surprisingly, God presses home the point by a change of tone from judgment to grace – offering in verse 12 a welcome home to converts from that old scapegrace Israel, before reassuring the house of Judah (not till six verses later!) that it too is included in the promise. But first, by implication, Judah will have shared the punishment, since both are seen returning from captivity: *together they shall come from the land of the north* (18).

Before we leave this passage we should notice the great vista opened up in verses 15–18. Characteristically, God is not content with short-term answers to a crisis, but looks on to perfection. In the short run, a band of exiles from Judah, with a sprinkling from the other tribes, would return from Babylon to Zion and struggle to rebuild their temple, their city and their way of life. But in the long run, all of this would be transcended. What is said here of the *shepherds* (*i.e.* rulers) and of the ark and the nations reveals the scale of this transformation, with God's people ideally governed (15), his

---

[12] In this passage the words translated 'faithless' and 'false' denote, respectively, turning (away) and treachery. On the skin-deep character of the reformation in Judah, see on ch. 11.

earthly throne no longer a mere ark but his entire city (note the astonishing boldness of v. 16); his Jerusalem the rallying point of all nations, now converted; and his divided Israel home and reunited. It brings us right into the era of the new covenant, and indeed to the new heavens and earth and the 'New Jerusalem' of Revelation 21 – 22, whose 'temple is the Lord God' (Rev. 21:22), and whose open gates admit 'the glory and the honour of the nations' (Rev. 21:26).

If so distant a prospect was worth unveiling to the old Israel, six centuries before Christ, it must be doubly relevant to us who have reached its foothills. Like our predecessors, we shall travel all the better for keeping the journey's end in view, especially now that the book of Revelation has pictured it for us even more invitingly than Jeremiah.

> Lift your eyes, ye sons of light!
> Zion's city is in sight;
> There our endless home shall be,
> There our Lord we soon shall see.

No glib response 3:19 – 4:4

To that glowing prospect there is no short cut. The rest of the passage spares us nothing of the pain, to God and man, of the breach within the family (3:19–20, 21–25) or of the deep repentance that must be the prelude to its healing (4:1–4). In plain terms, we must accept that the Lord is not for sharing, nor his laws for bending. Everything unreal must go,[13] and every moral compromise (4:1–2). In pictorial terms, more evocatively, 4:3–4 insists that there can be no spiritual harvest from hearts that stay unploughed, and no circumcision worth the name which leaves the will untouched. The law itself had said the same about this rite (Dt. 10:16), and in a scathing oracle Jeremiah 9:25–26 will rank Judah among the heathen because they are 'uncircumcised in heart'. The New Testament takes up both these analogies: that of the fallow ground, in the parable of the sower (Mk. 4:3–20), and that of the true circumcision, in Romans 2:25–29 (*cf.* Phil. 3:2–3; Col. 2:11–14).

---

[13] Not least, the double-talk which blurred the distinction between Yahweh and the gods. The Heb. of 3:14 reserves for him alone the relationship of 'husband/lord' (Heb. 'Baal') which Canaan's Baal usurped; and v. 24 accordingly gives Baal the derogatory nickname 'Bosheth' ('Shame'), which the OT likes to fling at him from time to time (*e.g.* 11:13).

Paul expounds it as implying the radical discarding of the self-life, in a death with Christ which issues in new life with him, as is now signified in Christian baptism.

Judgment from the north   4:5 – 6:26

If chapter 2 spelt out the betrayal of love, and 3:1 – 4:4 the cost of true repentance, the next three chapters bring the threat of judgment to the very doors. There is such an atmosphere of alarm here, that some writers have isolated the seven or eight most agitated poems as springing from Jeremiah's personal foreboding of invasion by the Scythians from central Asia, whose horsemen, according to Herodotus,[14] were terrorizing the Middle East at the time when Jeremiah was first prophesying. In the event, however, although the Scythians raided Ashkelon of the Philistines, there is no sign that they set foot in Judah, and it is plausible to suggest that consequently Jeremiah's hearers, and even he himself, concluded that he was a prophet whose predictions failed.

> Behold, they say to me,
> 'Where is the word of the Lord?
> Let it come!' (17:15).

Or again,

> O Lord, thou hast deceived me,
> and I was deceived;
> thou art stronger than I,
> and thou hast prevailed (20:7).

But while Jeremiah may well have been sensitized to the terrors of war through the Scythian threat, and may have expected these early

---

[14] Herodotus, *The Histories*, I, 104–106 (Translated by A. de Sélincourt, Penguin Classics, ²1972, pp. 84–85).

oracles to be fulfilled at any moment, the fact remains that God's word through him not only made no mention of the Scythians, but decisively excluded them at certain points.[15] It was Babylon, a generation later, which would bring all this to pass.

The invasion oracles   4:5ff., *etc.*, to 6:26

These vivid, urgent visions, breaking surface at irregular intervals in this group of chapters, are interspersed with divine comments of increasing length. The visions come thick and fast in chapter 4, bombarding us with the terrors of invasion; then in chapters 5 and 6 the balance between event and comment alters, as God builds up the case against his people, punctuating it only with the last three visions of the coming ordeal.

The visions (to look at these first on their own) are breathless with fear and confusion. Order and counter-order in the first poem and the last-but-one betray the fast-deteriorating scene, as the refuge turns into a death trap:

> ... fall back on the fortified cities.
> Raise the signal – To Zion! (4:5–6, NEB).

But then,

> *Flee for safety ... from the midst of Jerusalem!*
> *... This is the city which must be punished ...* (6:1, 6b).

Finally nowhere is safe:

> *Go not forth into the field,*
>   *nor walk on the road;*
> *for ... terror is on every side* (6:25).

Then again, subjectively, it would be hard to find a sharper description of uncontrollable inner turmoil than that of 4:19:

> *My anguish, my anguish! I writhe in pain!*
>   *Oh, the walls of my heart!*
> *My heart is beating wildly;*
>   *I cannot keep silent;*
> *for I hear the sound of the trumpet,*
>   *the alarm of war.*

[15] *E.g.*, by the mention of chariots (4:13) and, especially, of siege operations (4:16; 5:17c; 6:6), which were no part of Scythian tactics.

Meanwhile the turmoil outside overwhelms us, first as a disorientating mêlée in which everything happens at once:

> *Disaster follows hard on disaster ...*
> *Suddenly my tents are destroyed,*
> *my curtains in a moment* (4:20).

Then, in the chilling contrast of the next vision (4:23ff.), all is silence: a darkened, quaking desolation, described in language that looks back to the primeval scene:

> *I looked on the earth, and lo, it was waste and void;*[16]
> *and to the heavens, and they had no light.*

But while the Genesis story was all expectancy, this is the opposite: an abandonment, a reversion and a divine unmaking:

> *I looked, and lo, there was no man,*
> *and all the birds of the air had fled.*
> *I looked, and lo, the fruitful land was a desert,*
> *and all its cities were laid in ruins*
> *before the Lord, before his fierce anger* (4:25–26).

The picture is so extreme that only our present forebodings of nuclear winter may seem to come within sight of it. But today we are near the end of a road that was always leading this way, only waiting for our expertise to complete it – for sin and folly are always creating wastelands, whether literally in the form of dust-bowls and ruins, or figuratively in reducing to a desert the *fruitful land* (26) of a personality, a relationship or a society.

In that general sense, then, this vision warns every age, from Jeremiah's to our own, that 'sin, when it is finished, bringeth forth death' (Jas. 1:15, AV). But (thank God) it speaks more personally although more searchingly than that: namely, of the Lord's *fierce temper* (26c) but also of his forbearance (*yet I will not make a full end* (27) – a promise repeated at 5:10, 18).[17] Both of these, the wrath as well as the mercy, reflect his intense commitment to us – both the seriousness with which he takes us ('O think me worth Thine anger

---

[16] Heb. *tōhû wābōhû*, as in Gn. 1:2.

[17] The abruptness of this assurance, coming in the midst of threats, highlights both the fact and the wonder of it. Some commentators, however, find this too surprising, and treat it as an insertion by a later hand. G. A. Smith goes so far as to remove the word 'not' from the clause (Smith, p. 110)!

...'[18]) and the determination to complete the work of grace that he has begun. So in fact the desert would blossom in due course in response to the Redeemer; so too our Lord foretold a shortened tribulation for the sake of the elect (Mt. 24:21–22). So, finally, the doom of our whole universe, portrayed in terms that outstrip even the present passage, will make way for the glory of new heavens and earth (2 Pet. 3:10–13).

With this, we might have expected the series of visions to cease, having brought us to the point at which destruction has nothing it can add. But much was to happen before that:

the flight of refugees,

> *they enter thickets; they climb among the rocks;*
> *all the cities are forsaken* (4:29);

the frantic diplomacy and its brutal rebuff,

> *In vain you beautify yourself.*
> *Your lovers despise you;*
> *they seek your life* (4:30–31);

the invaders' alien tongue and voracious appetite,

> *They shall eat up your harvest ..., your flocks ...,*
> *your vines and your fig trees* (5:15–17);

then the siege of precious Jerusalem,

> *The comely and delicately bred I will destroy,*
> *the daughter of Zion* (6:2, with 1–8);

finally a beaten people, whose 'hands fall helpless',

> *anguish has taken hold of us,*
> *pain as of a woman in travail* (6:22–26).

The why and wherefore of these oracles in chapters 4 – 6

Interspersed with the visions of invasion are reflections and pronouncements – only a sentence or two at first, but growing in length – on the reasons for these desperate measures. So we return to the start of the series:

[18] John Donne, 'Good Friday, 1613, Riding Westward', in Peter Levi (ed.), *The Penguin Book of English Christian Verse* (Penguin Books, 1984), p. 82.

41

Chapter 4: the logic and limits of the judgment

Jeremiah is quick to protest at the very first of the oracles: *Ah, Lord God, surely thou hast utterly deceived this people and Jerusalem, saying, 'It shall be well with you'...* (4:10). It is the first of many glimpses into his troubled mind;[19] and his surprise at his own vision of verses 5–9 chimes in with the New Testament's dictum that such prophecies came not by the impulse of man but from God (2 Pet. 1:20–21). As for the glib assurance, *It shall be well* (lit. 'peace'), which had taken him in, he was on guard after this against easy speeches that had no roots in moral realities – 'saying, "Peace, peace," when there is no peace' (6:14). What *was* from God (*Now it is I who speak* ...,4:12b) would not heal 'the wound of [his] people lightly' (*cf.* 6:14a).

The next interjection, from God himself, put the blame where it belonged, and where, as often as not, it still belongs collectively:

> *Your ways and your doings*
> *have brought this upon you* (4:18)

(yet the book of Job warns us not to jump to this conclusion over individuals; still less, to draw comparisons – *cf.* also Lk. 13:1–5). His comment in verse 22 goes to the root of the fatal 'ways' and 'doings' of verse 18, diagnosing a state of monumental folly:

> *For my people are foolish,*
> *they know me not;*
> *they are stupid children,*
> *they have no understanding.*
> *They are skilled in doing evil,*
> *but how to do good they know not.*

As in Proverbs, the foolish are not the thick-headed but the wrong-headed, who may have plenty of sophistication (that worldly parody of wisdom[20]) but know nothing ultimately worth knowing (*they know me not*), and do nothing ultimately worth doing (*to do good they know not*). Good, in Scripture, is not only plain and simple ('very near you', Dt. 30:14): it has heights and depths which we must be taught even to see (as in, *e.g.*, the Sermon on the Mount) and inspired to love and do.

---

[19] In particular, chs. 12 – 20 have been called 'The Confessions of Jeremiah', in view of the protests and prayers they contain.

[20] 'Skilled' is lit. 'wise'. In the wrong hands it can describe even the 'crafty' (2 Sa. 13:3).

After this, and after the vision of a deserted landscape in 4:23–26,[21] the saving clause in verse 27, '*yet I will not make a full end*', shines very brightly. It is a constant theme, not only here (repeated at 5:10, 18; 30:11) but throughout the prophets. Without it the Old Testament would not have been worth writing, and the New Testament would never have materialized. Its context here of a silent, devastated world makes the point that only God's 'Yet ...' has rescued or will rescue anything at all from the battlefield that we have made of his creation.

Chapter 5: Jerusalem the brazen

Now, after the Lord's terse comments in chapter 4 between one disastrous vision and the next, chapters 5 and 6 take us behind the scenes, to face the facts which prompt the question of 5:7, *How can I pardon you?*

Jeremiah involves us in his tantalizing search of Jerusalem for one just man, as his hopes are dashed by the poor and then the great. His later chapters will bring to light a handful of staunch characters,[22] but the point of this passage is, first, that to find one such man is to find a needle in a haystack; and secondly, that Jerusalem is as far gone in iniquity as Sodom, if not further. Sodom, after all, was set a higher condition of reprieve than this: to muster ten just men, not one; and while Jerusalem is not accused of Sodom's particular depravity, her speciality was to sin against the light and against grace: aping the heathen in their blindness and the stallions in their lust (5:7–9). We may wonder whether these apostates had, like us, coined terms to dignify these trends as new theology and new morality. They sound modern enough in their airy dismissal of the wrath and word of God:

> He will do nothing! ...
> The prophets are but wind ... (5:12–13, NIV).

God's sharp reply exalts the self-fulfilling power of a true prophetic word, described here with strong simplicity as *my words in your mouth*' (14). Such an oracle will be like a match to a bonfire (14)

---

[21] See the comments on that vision, p. 40f.

[22] *E.g.*, Baruch his scribe (36:4ff.), Ebed-melech his rescuer (38:7ff.), the family of Shaphan (26:24, *etc.*), and others who spoke up for him in 26:16, 17, *etc.* It is possible, of course, that before the discovery of the book of law in 622, none of these men had been awakened.

43

— yet not in the fatalistic manner of a magician's curse, for it is always God himself who fulfils his word; and it carries within it, up to the last moment, an implied appeal or warning which may yet avert its threat (*cf.* 18:5ff.). Even apart from repentance, verse 18 speaks of royal mercy (as at 4:27; 5:10), while the poetic justice of verse 19 is unanswerable.

If we noticed a modern trait at verse 12, in the people's refusal to take God's anger seriously, verses 20–22 provide another foretaste of our age, which is determined not to give him credit for his creation. While Judah's contemporaries peopled the universe with gods, and Judah followed suit and worshipped them, our secular society thinks it enough to find out the mechanisms of the world and personify them as though they were its architect. C. S. Lewis's offer of a hymn for those who think this way may put matters more sharply than they themselves would, but the prophets too had a sense of the ridiculous as well as of the tragic.

> Lead us, Evolution, lead us
> Up the future's endless stair:
> Chop us, change us, prod us, weed us,
> For stagnation is despair:
> Groping, guessing, yet progressing,
> Lead us nobody knows where.[23]

With verse 25 the practical penalties of this blindness to the Creator, and the moral reasons for it, come into view. As for its penalties,

> *Your iniquities have turned these [blessings] away,*
> *and your sins have kept good from you.*

What Judah forfeited by defying God, modern man forfeits too: both directly, by looking to nature, not the God of nature; and indirectly, by being caught up in the race to use up everything within reach, in season and out of season (in contrast in the restraints and rhythms implied in v. 24).

As for the reasons for this blindness, they are basically moral, not intellectual: *your iniquities ... and your sins* (25), spelt out in verses 26–29 in terms of social wrongs against the poor – adding this dimension to that of the idolatry and adultery of verses 7–8 and of the earlier chapters.[24]

---

[23] C. S. Lewis, *Poems* (Bles, 1964), p. 55. There are five more verses.

[24] 2:34–35 ('the lifeblood of guiltless poor') is the only previous reference to sins of oppression.

JEREMIAH 4:5 – 6:26

So the chapter can only end with judgment. Notice how this is presented to us: not by flat assertions but by unanswerable questions. Early in the chapter the hope, *that I may pardon her* (1c) faded into *How can I pardon you?* (7); and now verse 29 has to echo the challenge of verse 9: *Shall I not punish them for these things?* It prepares us for the desolating close of the chapter in yet another searching question, led up to step by step by the spectacle of false prophets, venal priests,[25] and a purring people. There remains only the dreadful finality of the cry, *What will you do when the end comes?* The 'end' is the end of the process, not some arbitrary closure. There is a straight line from apostasy to disaster, from sin to death.

Chapter 6: 'They cannot listen'

The invasion oracle of 6:1–5 foresees Jerusalem as no longer a refuge (as at 4:6) but a trap, encircled by an enemy s oiling for the kill. Worst of all, this is from the Lord (6), and the rest of the chapter gives reason after reason why this must be so. In the first place, the city's wickedness is nothing slight ot superficial (7). Like the evil treasure from an evil heart, as our Lord put it (Lk. 6:45), it comes from deep within her – whether it should be pictured here as a spring which gushes up,[26] or, as the Hebrew more strongly suggests, as the cool waters of a well or cistern.[27] The thought of her keeping her iniquity as fresh as drinking-water is all the more telling for its irony – like the picture in Proverbs 4:16 of those devoted evildoers who 'cannot sleep unless they have done wrong'. We may be reminded of the care lavished in our own day on presenting and practising an 'alternative morality', and may be warned, with Jerusalem (8), *lest I be alienated from you ...* Yet the bitter word used for 'alienated' carries a reminder of the wrench that such a judgment means for God. It is eloquently brought out in NEB's paraphrase: 'lest my love for you be torn from my heart ...'

Secondly, Jerusalem's wickedness is the sin of a closed mind:

> *they cannot listen;*
> *behold, the word of the Lord is to them an object of scorn* (10b)

[25] The phrase 'at their direction' (31) is lit.'at their hands' (*cf.* 1 Ch. 25:2, 3, 6, 'under the direction of ...'). A just possible alternative to 'rule' is 'scrape' (*sc.* money into their hands), as in Jdg. 14:9, where Samson scrapes honey from the lion's skeleton. This would make the priests literally venal; but something of the same spirit is implied in the normal translation, where the priests take their cue from those who pander to the public mood.

[26] *Cf., e.g.,* AV, NIV.

[27] *Cf.* RSV, NEB, JB, GNB.

– and this is the mood of virtually every individual:

> Go over what is left of Israel's vineyard,
> scan her as a gardener scans twig after twig;
> is there a man whom I can warn ...? (6:9–10, Moffatt).

It confirms the findings of the famous search for a righteous man in 5:1–5, and the conclusion in 5:31 that 'my people', fed with false religion, 'love to have it so'.

For, thirdly, the closed mind produces a calloused conscience, vividly revealed in answer to the question, *Were they ashamed when they committed abomination?*, *No, ... they did not know how to blush* (15).

Even at the level of common sense, fourthly, there is no helping these people – for what can you do with folk who will not even ask the way when they are lost?

> *Stand by the roads, and look,*
> *and ask for the ancient paths,*
> *where the good way is; and walk in it,*
> *and find rest for your souls* (16).

But to them, *ancient* means only 'obsolete', not a path well tried or, indeed, eternal (as in David's 'lead me in the way everlasting'[28]); and *good* has no appeal, even though *the good way* promises firm going and a path that arrives. As for the compassionate offer of *rest for your souls*, it is brushed aside – for as sinners we do not take kindly either to God's diagnosis of our restless state or to his remedy for it. That remedy, both here and in our Lord's quotation of the last line (Mt. 11:29), is no rest-cure but a redirection: the blessed relief of stepping out along the right way. Jesus interprets this in personal terms of walking with him as his working partners ('my yoke upon you') and his pupils ('learn from me').

After the boorish reaction to these divine overtures, in the reiterated *We will not* ... (16b, 17b), it is a shock to find that these are studiously religious people, sparing no expense to offer God the best of everything (20) – everything, that is, but love. But since many prophets report the same phenomenon (we return to it in the next chapter), we may wonder whether it has any modern counterpart – whether, for example, our own religiousness is

---

[28] Ps. 139:24, where 'everlasting' is the same word, *'ōlām*, as 'ancient' here.

conceivably as cold as Judah's, to provoke again God's penetrating question of verse 20 (NEB): 'What good is it to me ...?'

That question carried its own answer, and the answer its own consequences, to be pictured in the invasion oracle of verses 22–26 (the last of the series[29]). Everything there reflects by its enormous scale the enormity of the offence. God's executioner will be no local force, but a world power, summoned from the ends of the earth. Its progress will be awesome and its arrival devastating, summed up in a phrase that will reverberate through the book and on into Lamentations: *terror ... on every side* (25).[30] The very words of verses 22–24, however, (to anticipate) will meet us again at the end of the book, spoken no longer against Judah but against Babylon itself! – for God is no respecter of persons or powers. See 50:41–43.

To their own threat, however, the people imagine that in possessing the temple they have a cast-iron answer: a guarantee which even God will have to honour. It will be the opening theme of chapter 7.

Meanwhile God has something new to say about the role of Jeremiah.

The prophet as God's assayer   6:27–30

This picture of the prophet's words as a refiner's fire makes its point not only by its vivid detail but by its tragic outcome. For it emerges that the people of Judah are not, so to speak, precious metal marred by some impurities, but base metal from which nothing of worth can be extracted.

The process of refining gold or silver, in those days, was to melt down lead with the rest of the metal, and then to direct a stream of air at the molten mass. This oxidized the lead, causing it to act as a flux to carry off the baser elements.[31] All this had been faithfully done, but to no avail (29):

---

[29] See above, p. 39.

[30] See 20:3–4 (where this phrase, *māḡôr missāḇîḇ*, becomes the ominous name given to the priest who tried to silence Jeremiah); see also 6:25; 20:10; 46:5; 49:29; La. 2:22.

[31] See the account in S. R. Driver, *The Book of the Prophet Jeremiah* (1906), p. 39, cited in Smith, p. 133.

> *The bellows blow fiercely,*
> *the lead is consumed by the fire;*
> *in vain the refining goes on,*
> *for the wicked are not removed.*

The conclusion agrees sadly with that of Jeremiah's search of Jerusalem in 5:1–5. In terms of the assayer's test,

> *Refuse silver they are called,*
> *for the Lord has rejected them (30).*

The distinctive point here is that the prophet not only speaks to a situation: in so doing he brings to the surface, and to a decision, what is latent in it, through the reactions that his words provoke. Paradoxically, it was the very 'failure' of his preaching that was the success of his assaying, unwelcome though the findings were. For it is not God's way to cover up what needs to come to light. That can be left to the popular preachers, whose epitaph is in verse 14.

Our Lord faced the same tragic outcome of his own outspokenness: 'If I had not come and spoken to them, they would not have sin; but now they have no excuse for their sin' (Jn. 15:22).

So the die is cast. The invader must come; the kingdom must fall.

The great temple sermon   7:1 – 8:3

Jeremiah may have preached on this subject more than once, since his dire warning in terms of the ruins of Shiloh (vv. 12, 14) meets us again in chapter 26, dated there in the reign of Jehoiakim (26:9). On that occasion, with no Josiah to protect him, the sermon nearly cost Jeremiah his life. It may be, however, that our present chapter, which is undated, belongs to that same troubled time, when Judah was caught between two warring empires, Egypt and Babylon, and was desperate for reassurance. While chapter 26 concentrates on the effect of the sermon on the hearers, chapter 7 is concerned with its contents in full, which clinch the predictions and reproaches of the previous chapters. The two sermons, or the two accounts of one sermon, complement and reinforce one another, pointing on to the blow which fell surely enough in 587.

The den of robbers   7:1–15

In Isaiah's day, people had trusted in a 'refuge of lies', telling themselves that the worst could never happen (Is. 28:15, 17). Here was something more blatant: treating the temple as a 'safe house' against not just the enemy but the Lord.

God's answer to the parrot-cry *The temple of the Lord* begins with an appeal to conscience (3–7), to reason (8–11) and to history (12–15).

The first of these appeals is as generous as it is searching, reopening the door of mercy which had been so often slammed back in God's face. But there could be no skimping of repentance, since the kind of mercy that turns a blind eye to evil is no mercy at all – as the victims of violence in verse 6 would need no telling, and as the apostates themselves would find out in the end *to [their] own hurt* (6c).

After this, the appeal to reason and to history in verses 8–15 mounts relentlessly to its climax. Its first step is to expose the nonsense – and the effrontery – of tearing up the ten commandments and turning up in church (10), as though saved to sin. The second, the *den of robbers* saying (11), brings out the greater nonsense of thinking to tie God's hands. The temple could only give sanctuary *as* a sanctuary. Let man take it over, and God will have left it. This is the point which Jesus made, when he quoted our verse 11 and went on to speak of *your house*, and to foretell its destruction.[32] (Has he cause at all, we may wonder, to use the words, 'your church'?)

It might still seem to them that God would shrink from the full logic of all this: therefore history is twice called in to refute the idea. The ruins of Shiloh (12–14) said all that needed to be said about the temple, and the disappearance of the northern tribes (summed up as *Ephraim*, 15) showed what Judah might expect. Moreover, Judah has already been pronouced the guiltier of the two kingdoms (3:11).

Wasted prayer   7:16–20

To tell Jeremiah not to pray for this people (16) was as logical as it was startling – for the context shows that to go on praying now against the fall of the kingdom might be natural but would in fact be wrong. This was not to imply, of course, a final rejection of

---

[32] Mt. 21:13; 23:38; 24:2.

Judah, for the still wider context reveals (*e.g.*, in ch. 31) that God had grace in store beyond and through the necessary judgment. But the glimpse in verse 18 of whole families assiduously worshipping the queen of heaven[33] shows how deeply pagan was the folk-religion of the time. No minor surgery would touch it.

Wasted sacrifice 7:21–26

If God's advice to Jeremiah not to waste time interceding (16–20) was a shock, his advice to Israel not to waste good meat in burnt-offerings knocked their stoutest prop away – for, short of human sacrifice, a burnt-offering was the highest bid, to their mind, that one could make for heaven's favour.

Nearly every prophet up to the Exile had to fight this outlook, so firmly was it held – a firmness which explains the vehemence of the language here. At first sight God seems to be disowning the whole idea of sacrifice; and some early critics of Old Testament history seized on this to drive a wedge between the Prophets and the Law. But in fact this way of speaking is the Bible's strongest way of comparing one thing with another – here, the moral with the formal – putting it not in the mild form of 'This is better than that',[34] but with the starkness of 'Not that, but this!'[35] In a famous saying, Hosea 6:6 puts the two ways of speaking side by side:

> For I desire steadfast love *and not* sacrifice,
> the knowledge of God, *rather than* burnt offerings.

The radiant counterpart of Jeremiah's invective against false sacrifice is seen at 17:26, where the prospect of an obedient Israel is crowned by a vision of worshippers flocking to Jerusalem, 'bringing burnt offerings and sacrifices, cereal offerings and frankincense, and bringing thank offerings to the house of the Lord'.

'If you have tears ...' 7:27–34

The call to Jerusalem to mourn (for the verbs of v. 29 are feminine, apostrophizing the city) suggests that God's words to Jeremiah in

---

[33] Perhaps the planet Venus, or the moon, or the goddess Ishtar/Astarte/Ashtoreth. The cakes of v. 18, offered to the deity, bore her image (44:19b) or were shaped as figurines. See 44:15–19 for the extraordinary tenacity of this superstition.

[34] *Cf.* 1 Sa. 15:22, 'Behold, to obey is better than sacrifice ...'

[35] *Cf.* Is. 1:11ff.; Am. 5:21ff.; Mi. 6:6ff.; Ps. 40:6ff.

verses 27ff. were still words for preaching, even though they foretold their own rejection. In passing, it may remind us how the greatest of prophets had to preach to the unhearing,[36] and how God could put these very circumstances to work for him – using Pharaoh's pride, for example, to enhance the glory of the Exodus, and Jewish bigotry to precipitate first the crucifixion of Christ and later the evangelization of the Gentiles.[37] It is something to bear in mind when we are tempted to assess the fruits of preaching by what we can immediately observe.

With verse 30 the indictment reaches a new intensity – which is saying something after the catalogue of broken commandments in verse 9! – with the crowning horror of child-sacrifice. What is most revealing, however, about the pagan outlook is the fact that this was thought to be a crowning piety. The very carefulness of God's repudiation of it – *which I did not command, nor did it come into my mind* (31) – tells its own tale of his people's darkened outlook.

All too appropriately, the place where parents tried to buy their own safety at their children's terrible expense, would become an open grave for their own remains (32–33). And its very name, *Topheth*, would be a curse, twice over: first, by being made to rhyme with *bosheth*, 'shame',[38] and hence pronounced as the word for 'spitting' (as in Job 17:6); and secondly, in that *the valley of the son of Hinnom* (gê' *ben-hinnōm*), where these rites took place', would become Jerusalem's burning refuse-tip, whose shortened name *gehenna* meets us as the New Testament's word for hell.

Verse 34, in its own way, finds another nerve to touch, with the memories of the carefree, cheerful sounds of a town at peace: sounds mocked by the echoing emptiness of ruins. Jeremiah returns to this thought more than once: see the references at 16:9.

In death dishonour, in life despair 8:1–3

The sermon ends (if these verses, still in prose, should be taken with ch. 7) on a note which takes away the last shreds of comfort for those whose hopes or memories are bound up with Jerusalem. There is fierce irony in the thought of the idolaters' end: as a scattering of

---

[36] Cf. Ex. 5:1–2; Is. 6:9ff.; Ezk. 2:3ff.; Mk. 4:11ff.; Acts 7:52, 57.

[37] Cf. Rom. 9:17; Acts 13:27; 28:26–28.

[38] Its original name may have been tephath (*t^epāṭ*), 'fireplace', where children were given as fire-offerings to Molech, *i.e.*, to Baal as king (*melek*, likewise distorted to 'rhyme' with *bosheth*). The wording of v.31, together with, *e.g.*, 19:5; Ezk. 16:21, refutes the idea that to be offered to Molech was a mere token ceremony. The victims were slaughtered and burnt.

bones, royal, ecclesiastical and plebeian, exposed to *the host of heaven, which they have loved and served*. Finally verse 3 plumbs new depths in terms of anguish (*cf.* the vain death-wish of Rev. 9:6), of divine rebuke (*this evil family*) and of the expulsion and break-up of a people. All that is contained in our modern term 'displaced persons', but carrying the added sting of blame, is the prospect they have chosen for themselves.

In miniature, this picture of despair, guilt and isolation portrays the pains of hell: of being finally told, 'Depart from me ...'[39]

An outpouring of rebukes, appeals, reflections, warnings and prayers
8:4 – 10:25

'What wisdom is in them?' 8:4–12

In matters spiritual and moral we act with a perversity which is quite unlike our common sense at other levels, let alone the impressive wisdom of our fellow creatures (even the bird-brained, 7a!). Physically, if we fall we pick ourselves up; if we miss the way we turn back. But spiritually, we can be incorrigible. Jeremiah's generation shows what madness can take hold of us, so that not content with wandering like sheep we go off at the gallop (6b); and theologically we may use our cleverness to trim the word of God (8) or to reject it outright (9). It makes little difference whether the scribes of verse 8 who tamper with Scripture, and the wise men of verse 9 who ignore it (in our terms, the high-handed theologians and the philosophers), are two kinds of people or only one – for there is nothing to choose between perverting Scripture and discarding it. In the act of 'mending the oracles of God' we deny their divine status.[40]

[39] Mt. 7:23.

[40] Some early biblical critics who viewed Jeremiah as totally opposed to the sacrificial system took v. 8 to be his rejection of those parts of the newly found book of the law which dealt with it, or even of the entire book. Against this, see the comments on 7:21–26 and on 11:1ff. Rather, the verdict of the present passage is akin to that of Jesus on the scribes and the 'wise and understanding' of his own day, in, *e.g.*, Mk. 7:9, 13; Lk. 10:21; Jn. 9:39–41.

The dire results of this arrogance (10–12) have already been described in 6:12–15, almost word for word. The repetition gives us another chance to take in the fact that a high calling, whether as scholar (8), preacher or ecclesiastic, gives no immunity against low temptations (love of money and popularity, 10, 11) or against hardening of the conscience (*they did not know how to blush*, 12). Nor will the penalties of these professional lapses be mild and civilized, but brutal (10) and disastrous (12b). Their sins have dragged the nation down; they will pay for them in full.

The sad necessity of judgment   8:13 – 9:22

Sad necessity is indeed the keynote of these varied oracles, starting with the very pictures that our Lord would use, of what awaits the barren fig tree or the useless vine-growth.[41] Whatever final mercy God may grant (and in Judah's case there would be a return from exile), and whatever patience he may show, he does not keep in office those who trifle with their calling. See, for example, his word to Eli (1 Sa. 2:30), to Israel (Mt. 21:43), to the church at Ephesus (Rev. 2:5) and to the individual (1 Cor. 9:27; 10:12). But remember, too, how good he was to the repentant Peter (Jn. 21:15ff.).

Meanwhile, for Jeremiah's Judah, everything in the next verses speaks of an impending situation too late to mend, as we listen to voices of panic and despair, to the clamour of invasion, and to God's ominous comparison of the enemy to *adders which cannot be charmed* (17).

If all this emphasized the iron necessity of judgment, the ensuing stanzas (8:18 – 9:3) bring out the pathos of it, in a mingling of cries from the prophet, the people and the Lord. Nothing could be more typical of the turmoil and cross-purposes of a strained relationship. On the people's side there is bitterness that God should stand aside in their hour of need:

> *Is the Lord not in Zion?*
> *Is her King not in her? (19)*
> *... The harvest is past, the summer is ended,*
> *and we are not saved (20).*

Verse 20's analogy is that of a double failure, first of the field-crops,

[41] Lk. 13:6–9; Mt. 21:18–19; Jn. 15:2.

then of the summer fruit, heralding a winter that hardly bears thinking about.

The Lord, for his part, has a counter-question that puts the blame where it belongs:

> *Why have they provoked me ...*
> *with their foreign idols? (19c)*
> *... for they proceed from evil to evil,*
> *and they do not know me ... (9:3b).*

But his voice also mingles with the heartbroken words of Jeremiah, who speaks on heaven's behalf as well as on his own,[42] in terms as poignant as God's outburst in Hosea 11:8, with that fourfold 'How can I ...?' and that divine confession, 'My heart recoils within me'. In the light of that, we need draw no sharp distinction between the human and divine laments of verses 18, 21–22, although 9:1–2 surely speaks with Jeremiah's personal voice and has companions elsewhere which speak undoubtedly from ground level (*cf.* Lam. 2:18–19; Ps. 55:6–8). But this man's steadfast career proves that in fact he answered his momentary thought of quitting with the equivalent of his Master's 'How can I give you up?' He might cry out,

> *O that I had in the desert*
> *a wayfarer's lodging place,*
> *that I might leave my people*
> *and go away from them! (9:2; 9:1, Heb.).*

But instead, he would later risk his money and his liberty for the sake of an inheritance in the doomed land, as a gesture of faith and hope (see ch. 32, and 37:11ff.). It was this sacrificial constancy that would earn him the famous (if pardonably inexact) comment of A. B. Davidson: 'Prophecy had already taught its truths; its last effort was to reveal itself in a life'.[43]

The fine character in *Pilgrim's Progress*, Mr Valiant-for-truth, was named in robust contrast to the men of 9:3 who, in AV's phrase, 'are

---

[42] The recurrent mention of 'the daughter of my people' suggests God as the speaker, though Jeremiah could use the words in a weaker sense. The closing expression of 9:3, 'says the Lord' (or, 'Oracle of Yahweh'), claims at least the end of the passage for God; and there is no clear break between it and the preceding verses.

[43] *Hastings' Dictionary of the Bible*, II, p. 576b.

not valiant for the truth upon the earth'.[44] Their poisonous double-talk becomes the main theme of the next verses, pungently expressed. Notice the allusion to Jacob the supplanter in verse 4 (3, Heb.), using his name as Esau did in Genesis 27:36; notice too the point made in verse 5 that lying has been a habit actually cultivated, and iniquity a strenuous pursuit.

Small wonder, then, that the scenes of judgment and ruin (7–22) are introduced with the question, *'for what else can I do?'* (7). At the same time, this judgment is seen as a partnership of refining (7) and requiting (9) – although 6:29 has made it clear that refining can be rejected. Even the Exile would be a purifying agent only by the grace of God and for the sake of his good name (Is. 48:8–11). Meanwhile these paragraphs spare us nothing of the desolation, the scattering, the weeping and – especially in verses 21–22 – the horror of a massacre, where, in a macabre metaphor, death not only prowls the streets but climbs the very windows; and where the fields too are strewn with his unnatural harvest.

The glitter and the gold   9:23–24

This saying – memorable and worth memorizing – comes with added force from its background of death and disaster just above; for we still need reminding that

> The glories of our blood and state
> Are shadows, not substantial things.[45]

In contrast, verse 24 presents a wealth of 'solid joys and lasting treasure', here and hereafter – for there is a nuance of practical good sense in the Hebrew here for *understands*,[46] while to 'know' God means life itself, even to eternity.[47] There is also contrast between the three fading glories of verse 23 and the three unfading ones of verse 24: the faithful love, justice and righteousness which are God's gifts to us before ever they are his expectations from us.

---

[44] *Cf.* RSV mg., NIV mg. But the cryptic Hebrew is probably best rendered in NIV (text): 'it is not by truth that they triumph in the land'. Truth here means primarily fidelity, sincerity.

[45] James Shirley, 'The glories of our blood and state', in Peter Levi (ed.), *The Penguin Book of English Christian Verse* (Penguin Books, 1984), p. 114.

[46] Heb. *haśkēl*. Keil's rendering, 'having understanding, and knowing me', brings out the distinction between the two verbs, and avoids the impression that we can 'understand' God.

[47] *Cf.* Jn. 17:3; Mt. 22:31–32.

A sacrament skin-deep   9:25–26

Already in 4:4, to say nothing of Leviticus 26:41 or Deuteronomy 10:16, God had made it plain that 'real circumcision is a matter of the heart'[48] – a fact which (we might add) applies equally to baptism. Here it is put with shocking candour, in lumping together Judah with 'lesser breeds without the law' – all of them alike circumcised meaninglessly in a rite which was thus no better than a mutilation (as Paul would put it in Phil. 3:2) or a mourner's disfigurement.[49]

Externalism, the great snare of the good churchman in every age, has seldom been more cuttingly attacked; yet it lives on!

Against idolatry: a polemic and a psalm   10:1–16

Why did so easy a target as idolatry need so many attacks in the Old Testament?[50] Verse 9 suggests one reason: the appeal of the visually impressive; but perhaps verse 2 goes deeper, in pointing to the temptation to fall into step with the majority. What 'everybody' does may be solemn nonsense (3ff., 14–15), and the fashionable thinkers *stupid and foolish* (8) theologically (which is where it matters); but it may take God to say so, and the godly to see it. This perception, incidentally, is one of the blessings of thoughtful worship, as seen in the psalm of verses 6–16. As it dwells on the incomparable Lord and his writ that runs world-wide (6–10); on his creatorship, as *the one who formed all things* (16); and on his commitment to his people, who mean everything to him, and he (by rights) to them (16b, a); so the glamour of gods that are made to measure disappears,[51] and the reproach of belonging to a minority becomes an honour.

It is interesting that the psalm to God is interrupted by a message to mankind in verse 11, arising out of the psalm's theology. And appropriately enough, this one verse is preserved in Aramaic, the

---

[48] The phrase is Paul's: Rom. 2:28–29.

[49] This seems to be the point of alluding to the desert-dwellers who 'cut the corners of their hair', if RSV, NIV mg., NEB mg., *et al.*, are correct. It was a mourning practice forbidden to Israel, along with other defacements, as unworthy of 'a people holy to the Lord': Lv. 19:27; Dt. 14:1–2.

[50] *E.g.*, Pss. 115:4–8; 135:15–18; Is. 40:19ff.; 44:9–20.

[51] Notice the word *hebel*, and its plural, in vv. 3, 8, 16, aptly translated in JB as 'a nothing', 'these Nothings'. This is the word with which Ecclesiastes dismisses all that is merely earthbound as 'vanity'.

language which became for centuries the common tongue of half the world.

Where judgment must begin! 10:17–22

Suddenly there is the sheer drop from the pinnacle to the depths: from the thought of Israel as God's own treasure (16) to the pathetic sight of her as a refugee (17) leaving the ruins for the road:

> Gather up your bundle from the ground,
> O you who dwell under siege!

– slung out (as it is brutally put in v. 18) not simply by the enemy but by God.

But God knew what he was doing – 'what else can I do?', 9:7 – and the cryptic close of verse 18 may view the ordeal as bringing them to their senses,[52] as indeed it largely did.

In the ensuing lament (19–21) we may be hearing the voice of Jeremiah himself as he identifies with his people (cf. 4:19ff., where 4:20 is close to our v. 20). Certainly along with the anguish there is the note of acceptance (I must bear it, 19b) and of placing the blame where it belongs – not on the Lord but on the leaders who ignore him (21) – which is a realistic attitude worthy of the prophet, and far from the negative and hasty reactions that are more natural and more sterile.

A confession and a plea 10:23–25

This final prayer is one to sharpen our perception in three areas at least: first, about our collective blindness on our own, or at any rate our limited field of vision as we pick our way with our eyes down, without even an agreed destination, let alone a route. Secondly, about our individual need to be rectified and schooled by God, seeing the deep affront to him (24b) of our unresponsiveness. Thirdly, standing back from verse 25, we see the difference between the quite proper prayer of the Old Testament for judgment on the infidel and the oppressor, and the prayer in this day of grace for their salvation. Philip Pusey's hymn, 'Lord of our life', puts it well:

---

[52] Lit. 'that they may *find* ' – leaving the object unsaid. A change of vowels would yield '... may be found' (Vg., cf. LXX); but JB keeps 'find' and supplies 'me' as the object (cf. Syr.). More drastic emendations underlie NEB, GNB.

THE COVENANT AS CATALYST

Grant us thy help, till foes are backward driven,
Grant them thy truth, that they may be forgiven.
Grant peace on earth, and after we have striven,
    Peace in thy heaven.

The covenant as catalyst 11:1 – 12:17

When the lost book of the law was found in the temple in Josiah's eighteenth year (621), the king had it read out to a great gathering in the temple court, and led his people in a renewed covenant 'to perform the words of the covenant that were written in this book'. The story can be read in 2 Chronicles 34:8ff., especially verses 29–33.

Our chapter arises, it seems, directly out of this, and gives a fascinating glimpse of the cross-currents beneath the surface of this great reform. King Josiah saw to it that it remained the established faith, 'all his days' (2 Ch. 34:33); but he could not change the hearts and habits of his people. This comes out in two ways here: first in the nation-wide idolatry that refused to be stamped out (9–17), and secondly, at the local level, in the conspiracy against Jeremiah's life by the men of his own village (18–23), apparently for prophesying in support of the reform.

The preaching mission 11:1–8

Looking closely at these verses we can be struck by the sudden cluster of expressions that echo the books of the law, especially Deuteronomy.[53] It is hard to resist the impression that the words of the great public reading were still ringing in the prophet's ears as God sent him on his preaching tour through *the cities of Judah and … the streets of Jerusalem* (6) with the uncompromising covenant as his text. A point that we may miss in verse 2 is that the hearers

---

[53] *E.g.*, 'the words of this covenant', vs. 2, 3, 6, 8, *cf.* Dt. 29:9 (8, Heb.); 'Cursed be the man … Then I answered, "So be it Lord"', vv. 3, 5, *cf.* Dt. 27:26; 'from the iron furnace', v. 4, *cf.* Dt. 4:20; 'walked in the stubbornness of his evil heart', v. 8, *cf.* Dt. 29:19 (18, Heb.).

themselves were meant to spread the message.[54] So the impact of the great central occasion was to be prolonged and to proliferate, instead of fading into the past, and the implications of it were to be spelt out where people lived. The whole exercise is thought-provoking, with its intended partnership of preacher and hearers, of the big day and the everyday, and with the fact that the only novelty it sought was that of reapplying long-forgotten truth.

The old rebellion   11:9–17

There is an initial puzzle about this passage, if the previous one reflects Josiah's reformation as it surely seems to. A concealed resistance to the king's drive against idolatry was all too natural, but while he was on the throne there was little chance of dedicating whole cities to strange gods, still less of filling Jerusalem with altars to Baal (13, see 2 Ch. 34:3–7). So what we find here is probably what came to the surface as soon as Josiah's son Jehoiakim gave a lead back to the old ways which we met in chapter 2.[55] What made it almost worse than a straight repudiation of the Lord was the bland idea that the Lord must share his *beloved* (15, poignantly!) with the rest of her lovers. Nowhere is it clearer than here (14–15) that in that case to feel at home in God's house, reassured by his sacraments and conscious of a great tradition (16), is to be totally deceived.

But in Jeremiah's education, the fact that the ancient covenant, so zealously enforced and widely preached, had once more left the people's heart untouched, may have begun to prepare him for the message of a new and deeper covenant to come. That promise (31:31ff.) would be the high point of his whole prophecy.

A murderous resolve   11:18–23

The clue to the violent reaction of Jeremiah's neighbours and family (*cf.* 12:6) may lie in the fact that Anathoth was a priestly village.[56] As such, it was hard hit by the reformation, which closed down all

---

[54] Both 'hear' and 'speak' (2) are plural imperatives. But v. 3 opens with a personal charge to the prophet.

[55] Compare vv. 12–13 with 2:28. On the popular feeling against Josiah's reforms, see again 44:15–19.

[56] Jos. 21:18; 1 Ki. 2:26.

local sanctuaries as the law demanded[57] (picture the outcry that would greet this action against one's local church!) and transferred their priests to lesser duties in Jerusalem (2 Ki. 23:8–9). That Jeremiah, son of a priest (1:1), should have said Amen to this (5c), must have branded him a traitor – not for the last time as he followed his conscience and his instructions (37:11–15; 38:1–6).

His fierce reaction to the plot (20) will shock us; but God upheld it, for it asked no more than justice. What pointed all unconsciously to 'a more excellent way' was of course the very expression that, to Jeremiah, sharpened dramatically his cry for vengeance:

> But I was like a gentle lamb
> led to the slaughter (19).

To us, this side of Calvary, his words cut quite the other way, since, as Peter unsparingly reminds us, 'to this you have been called, because Christ also suffered for you, leaving you an example ...' (1 Pet. 2:21, cf. Is. 53:7).

Nowhere is the old way more gently or more radically challenged than by that example.

The prophet's outburst   12:1–4

This is one of many cries of 'Why?' and 'How long?' in the Old Testament[58] – to which God's answer is never philosophical, as though he owed us explanations, but always pastoral, to rebuke us, reorientate us or reassure us. Here, when we include the long view of the closing verses (14–17), there will be something of all three.

It was wise of Jeremiah (and an example worth remembering) to precede what he could not grasp with what he could not deny: namely, *Righteous art thou*. His 'Why?' could then take its proper place and tone: troubled but teachable. Yet we can be grateful that we hear the very human, urgent voice that speaks here, exaggerating the gloom as we tend to do in bad times (do *all* who are treacherous thrive, 1?), welcoming too personally the thought of retribution (3b, echoing 11:19), and slipping from his general concern (*How long will the land mourn?* 4a) into preoccupation with his private hurt (4d).[59]

---

[57] See Dt. 12, throughout.

[58] *E.g.*, Jb.; Pss. 22; 73; Hab.

[59] 'He will not see our latter end' was probably a taunt against Jeremiah rather than God. The prophet of doom, they are boasting, will be robbed of his satisfaction!

A bracing reply   12:5–6

For our own good, self-pity must be banished, and facts be faced: hence the tone of verse 5:

> *If you have raced with men on foot, and they have wearied you,*
> *how will you compete with horses?*

– hence, too, the bad news of verse 6, now broken to him, that not only his village but his own family is out for his blood.

So the pace has already quickened, and the question is now not Jeremiah's 'How long?' but the Lord's '*How will you compete ...? How will you do ...?*' Faithful friend that he is, the Lord knows when to be unsparing with us, and when to relent.[60] The sensitive Jeremiah rose to the challenge, not without loud cries of protest in the course of the next eight or nine chapters (sometimes called his 'Confessions', sometimes his 'Gethsemane'). The result of this hard training can be seen in his fortitude, right through to the end of his comfortless career.

A larger context   12:7–13

The second part of God's reply is remarkable, saying in effect, 'Your tragedy is a miniature of mine.'

This still speaks to many of our most wounding situations. The pain of ingratitude, indifference, disappointment; desertion by a spouse; defiance by a son or daughter, are things that God himself knows very well.[61] To get the point of verses 7ff., we may need (for a start) to emphasize the possessives:

> *I have forsaken* my *house,*
> *I have abandoned* my *heritage ...*
> My *heritage has become to me*
> *like a lion in the forest,*
> *she has lifted up her voice against me* (7–8).

It is, in measure, a true parallel, since the family's rejection of Jeremiah sprang directly from the nation's rejection of his Master. There is even some parallel between the prophet's and the Lord's indignation against their false friends – for although we need to

---

[60] Heb. 12:3–12; 2 Cor. 1:3–11.
[61] *Cf.*, *e.g.*, Is. 1:2; Ho. 2:5ff.; 11:1–4; Jn. 13:18.

understand the words *therefore I hate her* (8c) in the sense of 'therefore I reject her', the entire passage announces wrath and retribution on the people and their land.

Yet grief keeps showing through, in the revealing expressions, *my heritage, my portion*; above all, *the beloved of my soul* (7, *cf.* 11:15). The other thing that needs saying is that the situation offered no alternative. God's *beloved* had turned vicious (7–8), his *vineyard* was already vandalized (10), his *heritage* no longer a prodigy among the nations but an oddity to be mobbed (9). (Does the church sometimes need to wonder whether it is conspicuous for its piety or for its plumage?)

It is generally we, not God, who struggle to preserve what we have ruined. But it is God who smites to heal; or, as he had put it to Jeremiah at the outset, who calls for demolition in order 'to build and to plant' (1:10). This brings us to the final verses.

The distant prospect 12:14–17

Jeremiah had asked about the justice of God's dealings with the wicked: now he is given a longer view. First, God's name for certain of them as *my evil neighbours* (14) leaves no doubt about their guilt and punishment. But then, surprisingly, he proposes to restore them to their lands,[62] out of compassion (15), and to offer them conversion and integration into his people (who have likewise, by implication, been repatriated). But there is no future for any nation otherwise (17).

It was a reassuring answer to the doubts that troubled Jeremiah, but a more generous one, perhaps, than he expected. It spoke in comparatively local and historical terms, but beyond these we can see from our vantage-point the breaking down of the party-wall between Jew and Gentile which the gospel was to bring,[63] and the prospect of 'a great multitude ... from every nation ... standing before the throne and before the Lamb ...' (Rev. 7:9).

At the same time, there is no concession to the old ways or the old gods – in our modern terms, to religious pluralism. As for their ways, the heathen must *diligently learn the ways of my people*; and as for their allegiance, they must *swear by my name ... even as they taught my people to swear by Baal* (16).

[62] *Cf.* 46:26 (Egypt); 48:47 (Moab); 49:6, 39 (Ammon, Elam).
[63] Eph. 2:11–22; Gal. 3:26–29.

If any doubt remained about the importance of the issue – whether for example it meant choosing merely between a higher religion and a lower, or in truth between nothing less than life and death – the final verse settles it as conclusively as the close of the Sermon on the Mount or the book of Revelation.[64]

Five variations on a dark theme   13:1–27

One of these collected messages, that of verses 18–19, dates itself fairly certainly in the reign of Jeconiah (598/7), but the rest may have been given at various times, with one theme in common: the prospect of defeat and exile.

The spoilt waistcloth   13:1–11

Here was an errand in sharp contrast to the hopeful one of 11:6. Then it had been a preaching tour with a call to renewal; now it is a solitary journey towards foreign parts and a foregone conclusion.

Whether this was a literal journey, twice over, to the distant river Euphrates,[65] or a journey of the mind (like some of Ezekiel's experiences), its point was very clear: that for Judah to have exchanged her close bond with the Lord (that they might *cling to me*, 11) for a commitment to a far-off heathen power, and to heathen gods near and far, was to deny her *raison d'être* (namely to be *for me a people, a name, a praise, and a glory*, 11, *cf.* Eph. 1:12). The process had rotted her spiritual fibre as surely as the riverside had ruined Jeremiah's linen cloth, leaving both alike *good for nothing* (7).

It was not of the Exile that God was speaking – for that would be in fact a purging – but rather of the policy which had looked to the

---

[64] Mt. 7:13–27; Rev. 22:6–19.

[65] The Heb. for the Euphrates is *p'rāṭ*, hence it has been tentatively suggested that Jeremiah was sent instead to Parah (Jos. 18:23), *i.e.*, Wady Farah near Anathoth, chosen as a symbol of Euphrates for its similarity of name, since two round journeys of some 500 miles each may seem excessive for so simple an experiment. The very excess, however, may have been part of the intended lesson, both of Judah's laboriously futile diplomacy in the past and of the long march that awaited her again.

Mesopotamian powers of Assyria and Babylon for help, from as long ago as Ahaz[66] and even Hezekiah,[67] and which had cultivated since then whatever were the gods that seemed to offer most.

To borrow words that would be written a thousand years later, this acted parable was saying, 'Thou hast made us for thyself ...' – for to seek fulfilment anywhere else is as bizarre (if we could see it) as Jeremiah's weary expedition and foredoomed experiment.

The wine jars   13:12–14

A popular saying makes a good springboard for a prophet – especially for springing a surprise! Here the tag evidently meant something optimistic, such as, 'The more you expect, the more you'll get,' or perhaps, 'It'll all come right in the end.'

Jeremiah's twist of it was a double one. He saw God's wine for them as grimly potent,[68] and every man (like *every jar*) filled with it, not merely to confusion but to destruction – all blindly smashing one another as though they were the jars[69] that their fancy dwelt on.

It could almost be a picture of our present world.

Fading light   13:15–17

To be overtaken by darkness on a mountain: that is the kind of plight which every moment is bringing nearer; yet there is still a trace of daylight left. This urgent message, amidst the uncompromising oracles that surround it, opens the door of escape for a brief minute, to remind us *why* the prophet has been speaking so unsparingly (on this, see 18:7–11). And not only why, but in what frame of mind: *my soul will weep in secret for your pride* (17). There is all the difference between this attitude and that of the merely scolding preacher, whose aggression or exasperation only aggravates the pride it meets. As the passage twice reminds us, the hearer's pride is the sure prelude to his fall (*cf.* Pr. 16:18) and his humiliation.

---

[66] 2 Ki. 16:7; Is. 8:5–8.
[67] Is. 39.
[68] *Cf.*, *e.g.*, Ps. 75:8; Rev. 14:10; 18:6.
[69] NIV's 'smashed wineskins' is unfortunate. A *nēbel* could equally be of earthenware (Is. 30:14; La. 4:2).

A royal dirge 13:18–19

Once again the tone is sad, though the facts are hard. It breathes the spirit of David's lament for Saul: 'How are the mighty fallen ...!' (2 Sa. 1:25, 27). The king in question is evidently the young Jeconiah/Jehoiachin, who is mentioned several times elsewhere in conjunction with the queen mother, with whom he was to go into exile in 597.[70] The threat to the cities of the Negeb (19) underlines the completeness of the defeat, since these at least, in the far south, might have hoped to remain unscathed.

In short, no-one is so high, nothing so venerable, nowhere so safe, as to be exempt when God sends in his agents of upheaval and destruction. To say, 'It couldn't happen here' is (as we are all finding out) not even plausible.

Disgrace for Jerusalem 13:20–27

After the 'beautiful crown' of verse 18 it is the *beautiful flock* (20) that must be mourned – for it is now Jerusalem,[71] with her citizens or her cities (19), whose turn it is to be addressed. Bitterness and shame dominate the passage: the gall of cultivating the powerful, only to be enslaved by them (21); and the humiliation of exposure to gloating and abuse (22b, 26). Under the savage metaphors the lesson is that a people that parts with its virtue – its morals, its integrity, its faith – will find itself not liberated, only cheapened: stripped of everything that gave it value and respect.

As for the protest, *Why have these things come upon me?* (22), the very asking of such a question by such a generation would show how *accustomed* (23) it had grown to decadence. Evil, not only fitting them like a glove, not only deep-dyed, was by now something they could no more change or wish to change than the colour of their skin (23):

> *Can the Ethiopian change his skin*
> *or the leopard his spots?*
> *Then also you can do good*
> *who are accustomed to do evil.*

---

[70] Je. 22:24–30; 29:2; 2 Ki. 24:12, 15. The queen mother's position was influential in Israel: *cf.* 1 Ki. 15:13; 2 Ki. 11:1, 3, and the regular recording of the names concerned. Jehoiachin's mother was Nehushta, of Jerusalem: 2 Ki. 24:8.

[71] She is addressed in the feminine singular, and named in 27b.

There was nothing for it but judgment (that is, the Babylonian Exile); yet the chapter ends by looking further on, with a 'How long?' which laments the process but will not be cheated of the outcome (27):

> How long will it be
> before you are made clean?

The same Lord, we are assured, 'disciplines us for our good, that we may share his holiness' (Heb. 12:10).

Drought upon drought, and worse to come
14:1 – 17:4

The drought described   14:1–6

In a few terrible verses the plight of every living thing confronts us, from the highest to the humblest, from the most organized to the most instinctive, for lack of what none of them can command, and what none can do without. On so fine a thread hangs all that we take for granted. Moreover, the word translated *drought* (1) is plural here, indicating a series of such disasters, each one leaving the survivors less able to face the next. If anything could drive a nation to its knees, this was it – the only question being whether it would be a response of panic or of penitence. The next two paragraphs supply the answer.

Strong intercession   14:7–9

Surely God (Jeremiah prays) cannot stand aloof from all this suffering, like some embarrassed passer-by who has no desire to get involved? There could hardly be a stronger set of pleas than those that the prophet pours out here: not only the reproaches of verses 8b–9a but the positive considerations that surround them, which are a model for any prayer of penitence. We notice the appeal to God's good name, not man's deserving (7a, *cf.* the glorious Ezk. 36:22–32); we hear the heartening epithets describing God as

66

Israel's *hope* and *saviour* (8a), and we note the reminder of the bond that exists already between the Lord and his own (9b). Like many passages from the Psalms, it puts into words what we ourselves may sometimes need to pray, but lack the confidence or knowledge to express.

The plea refused   14:10 – 15:4

What are we to make of this reply? Not, as we have seen,[72] that God has gone back on his covenant, but that there is no going back on this generation's punishment. What will emerge in the end is another matter – see the glimpse of it in, *e.g.*, 16:14–15 – but meanwhile Judah can expect not only the drought it is already suffering, but the full force of *sword, … famine, and … pestilence* (12). The trouble is that Jeremiah's heartfelt intercessions are out of key with the whole tone and temper of his people, who *have loved to wander* (10), and whose fasts, prayers and offerings (12) spring from no repentance. He may speak as if for them in the prayer that ends the chapter –

> *We acknowledge our wickedness, O Lord …*
> *We set our hopes on thee* (14:20, 22)

– but the Lord's reply in 15:1–4 is more devastating than ever, for he looks for something more than the lone voice of an intercessor:

> *Send them out of my sight, and let them go! And when they ask you,*
> *'Where shall we go?' you shall say to them, 'Thus says the Lord:*
> > *"Those who are for pestilence, to pestilence,*
> > *and those who are for the sword, to the sword;*
> > *those who are for famine, to famine,*
> > *and those who are for captivity, to captivity."'*
> (15:1–2)

So the three scourges of 14:12 are joined by a fourth, captivity; and from here to 17:4 one or another of them will keep looming up, variously expressed.

In passing, note the legacy of King Manasseh in all this (15:4) – for Scripture faces us with the solidarity between the generations, for

---

[72] *E.g.*, on 3:11ff.; 4:27; 13:27b.

good or ill.[73] If our minds cavil at this, our instincts are at home with it, in the pride, shame, or desire to make amends, which our predecessors' acts may still evoke in us. The monstrous Manasseh found personal forgiveness (2 Ch. 33:12–13), but his legacy remained, both in the unrequited crimes of his regime against the innocent, and in the sins he had taught his people to embrace.[74] Those crimes and sins were not to be disclaimed now as a burden that the new generation should not be saddled with, as the popular tale of woe made out ('The fathers have eaten sour grapes, and the children's teeth are set on edge', 31:29, *cf.* Ezk. 18:2). The protest had in fact a hollow ring, shown up in a single sentence: 'You have done worse than your fathers' (16:12).

Interlude: a new dirge for Jerusalem   15:5–9

We can only appreciate the spirit of this lament for the unlamented (5), which is nevertheless relentless (6b) in its catalogue of judgments, if we are quite clear that God is the only source of good, and is man's only rightful lord.

> To turn aside from thee is hell,
> To walk with thee is heaven.

If there were anything arbitrary in his demands or invitations, if they were anything less than 'the things which belong unto thy peace' (as another lament for Jerusalem would put it[75]), then we might be stumbled by the carnage of verses 7–10. But sin's effects and heaven's judgments are but two sides of the same coin, whether they are expressed as in verse 6 –

> *You have rejected me ...;*
> *so I have stretched out my hand against you*

– or in our Lord's equally conclusive words,

> How often would I have gathered your children together ... and you would not! Behold, your house is forsaken and desolate.[76]

---

[73] *Cf.*, *e.g.*, Ex. 20:5–6; 1 Ki. 11:12; 14:10–11; 2 Ki. 19:34.

[74] 2 Ki. 21:1–16; 2 Ch. 33:1–20.

[75] Lk. 19:42, AV. 'Thy peace', using the rich word shalom, is the expression employed also at the end of our v. 5.

[76] Mt. 23:37–38.

A second interlude: personal protests and a challenging reply   15:10–21

Already Jeremiah had wrestled with God over the plot to murder him (11:18ff.) and over the thriving of the wicked (12:1–4). This new series of outbursts and pleadings[77] is precious to us for the light his candour throws on his prophesying: as a compulsion to speak what God directed, not what he desired or even prayed for (11). The strength of his revulsion reveals his temperament as well: for he was no masochist, enjoying affliction for its own sake, or half in love with death (instead, *take me not away*, 15). Nor was he a natural 'loner': it was only through God's hand on him that he *sat alone* (17) with no heart for laughter. His wry comment in verse 10 shows how unjustly but how heartily he was disliked: *I have not lent* (who loves a money-lender?) *nor have I borrowed* (who loves a debtor?), *yet all of them curse me.*

Most revealing of all, however, is his disappointment with his message, and consequently even with his Master, whose words were once a joy to him (16), but now a bitter pill. Whether he resented most the distastefulness of his predictions, or their seeming failure to materialize,[78] or the persecution they provoked, we are not to know. What we do have is a reply which (like the Lord's reply to Job) answered not the complaints but the complainer. That in itself was comment enough on where the trouble lay.

Broadly, God's reply was first bracing (19), then heartening (20–21). The challenge of verse 19 reiterates the verb for *turning*: first, in repentance, his turning back to God, and God's restoring of him (another aspect of the same verb) – for this relationship is everything, and it must be unspoilt. As God's spokesman, he must allow himself no alloy of faithless thoughts and words (19):

> *If you utter what is precious, and not what is worthless,[79]*
> *you shall be as my mouth.*

Notice that there is no release from his calling: only a renewing of it.

---

[77] See also 17:14–18; 18:19–23; 20:7–18.

[78] See the opening comments on the section, 'Judgment from the north' (4:5 – 6:26), p. 38.

[79] Or, 'If you separate the precious from the worthless' – which could refer either to the prophet's words, as above, or more generally to his function as God's assayer and tester (6:27ff.).

And this is sharpened by the remaining repetitions of *turn* in this verse:

> *They shall turn to you,*
> *but you shall not turn to them.*

Popular or unpopular (which had been a burning issue for this thin-skinned man), a prophet must be – and must still be – as uncompromising as the truth itself.

After this, the heartening promises of verses 20–21 remind Jeremiah of his opening call, almost word for word (*cf.* 1:18–19). They offer nothing easy. But the strength that they speak of, and the undefeated outcome, will be the glory of Jeremiah's maturity.

The message embodied   16:1–13

It is one thing to grow eloquent over a dire prospect for a wicked nation; quite another thing to taste the medicine itself. To ask this of Jeremiah, denying him the cherished gift of wife and children (an almost unthinkable vocation at the time), and then to isolate him from sharing the occasions of sorrow and joy around him (5, 8), was the measure of God's intense concern to get the message across.[80] *This*, and worse (the message ran), was what life would soon be like for everyone: with families wiped out, reduced to carrion (4–5), and existence so bleak without God's *peace* and *love* and *mercy* (5b), that it would lose even the faintest glow of human warmth: *the cup of consolation* in bereavement (6–7), let alone *the voice of mirth and the voice of gladness, the voice of the bridegroom and the voice of the bride* (9).[81]

The popular reaction to all this (10) – the tone of injured innocence, the *Why?*, the *What is our iniquity?* – is typically human and is proof enough of the condition that cried out for judgment. When we read God's answer (11ff.), to find the old, familiar charge of idolatry, that lesson ever taught and never learnt, we get some insight into Judah's insensitivity to God, and her inverted scale of values, whereby the first commandment was the last to be considered. But to be amazed at her tolerance of other gods is to be no less amazed at a generation – our own – which prides itself on

---

[80] Isaiah and Ezekiel were also given roles to act out at great cost to themselves. See, *e.g.*, Is. 20; Ezk. 24:15–24.

[81] This haunting expression, a witness to Jeremiah's responsiveness to atmosphere, is almost a refrain in the book: see 7:34; 25:10; and, joyfully at last, 33:11.

religious pluralism and is embarrassed at the exclusive claims of Christianity.[82]

A greater exodus   16:14–18

Resourcefully, God varies the announcement of captivity by promising a glorious end to it (14–15). But having done so, he subtracts nothing from the ordeal itself, for the punishment must be meted out in full (16–18).[83] The famous opening to Isaiah 40, while using a different word for 'double', brings out the positive side of this thorough retribution, in the assurance that all was settled now without remainder – an assurance on the plane of temporal punishment which (we may add) would one day be outmatched by the 'full, perfect and sufficient ... satisfaction' for sin made on our behalf by our Redeemer.

A still greater prospect   16:19–21

The thought of God's proven reality, over against the phantom gods of heathenism, opens Jeremiah's eyes to foresee the day when far-flung peoples will realize the hollowness of their religions and turn to the Lord. If this seems almost too remote a hope, it can reawaken our wonder at the fact that most of us who read these words are drawn *from the ends of the earth* (19), as part of their fulfilment.

Anticlimax!   17:1–4

Coming straight after the vision of converted pagans, the fact that Judah 'in his blindness' – self-chosen – 'bows down to wood and stone', can mean only one thing: that Jeremiah's generation is beyond recall. The land is comprehensively defiled (2–3), and the people's heart has guilt not only written all over it but etched into it, engraved (1) beyond erasure.

Did this language about the impenitent heart prepare Jeremiah

---

[82] See, *e.g.*, Jn. 14:6; Acts 4:12; 17:30–31; 1 Tim. 2:5–6.

[83] 'Doubly recompense' (18) may be a strong expression for a thorough punishment, or alternatively the word *mišnēh* ('double') may mean the 'equivalent' of the offence. See Harrison, p. 105, referring to D. J. Wiseman's article 'Alalah' *NBD*, p. 24a (*IBD*, p. 30a).

for the searching of his own heart (see the comment on v.9) and for the great promise of heart-obedience in 31:33?

The two ways for mankind   17:5–11

Placed immediately after the pair of prophecies which have reversed the usual roles of Gentile and Jew, this refreshingly different kind of passage drives home the fact that all of us alike, simply as human, are answerable to God, who has no arbitrary rules. The analogies (*like a shrub ... like a tree ... like the partridge*); the beatitude (7); above all, the talk of two rival ways of life, recall the wisdom writings, particularly the wisdom-psalm which opens the Psalter (which may be indebted to this passage). Further back, there stands the law (especially perhaps the rediscovered law-book), which prescribed a ceremony of declaiming the curses and the blessings which God's people must choose between.[84]

Looking more closely at the passage, we are struck by the inwardness of the character studies in verses 5–8. The pivot-word is *trust*, for everything will turn on where one's heart is. The worldly man, wasting his hopes on what is secondary and shifting, cannot flourish – for verses 5–6 describe above all the man himself. Outwardly he may be doing very nicely (as Jeremiah had complained in 12:1–2), but in himself he is sadly stunted. Elsewhere there may be 'showers of blessing', but in his spiritual desert he remains untouched (6a). The truth about that desert, the godless world, is summed up with masterly brevity in the three features of 6b: thirst, loneliness and sterility.

In God's book, the only alternative to *cursed* is *blessed*: there is no middle ground. The key to it here, as in the New Testament, is faith; and the virtual repetition in verse 7 of the first line by the second (preserved in RSV: *... who trusts in the Lord, whose trust is the Lord*) highlights the living object and content of this faith: the person of the Lord. Given this, the contrast with the desert shrub must follow, starting with the roots, for nourishment; up to the

---

[84] Dt. 27:11–26; 28:1ff.; 30:15ff.

leaves, for health; culminating in the fruit that makes the tree itself a blessing. Here again, this may or may not show in outward circumstances: it is the man himself (7–8a) who is described, seen as heaven sees him.

But only heaven sees us as we really are, and can deal with us as we should be dealt with (9–10). The wisdom writers point out that a man's thoughts and even words are deep, and may give little of him away;[85] but verse 9 goes further, to see deep trouble here. The word *deceitful* has echoes of Jacob the devious (*cf.* Gn. 27:36), while the single word for *desperately corrupt* (RSV) might be better understood as 'desperately sick' (RV, NEB).[86] Jeremiah shows us how to react to this diagnosis: not with self-defence but with the urgent 'Heal me, O Lord' of verse 14.

True to the 'wisdom' approach, verse 11 sums up the man who sells his soul for what he cannot keep,[87] in a single word. Jesus went further, to apply that word 'fool' not only to the unscrupulous but to the simply selfish (Lk. 12:20–21).

A burst of praise and a cry of pain 17:12–18

To his contemporaries, Jeremiah seemed morbidly negative, belittling everything from the temple downwards and longing for the day of doom. But here we glimpse 'the zeal of thine house'[88] which had inspired the tirade of chapter 7 against reducing the temple to a talisman and a thieves' nest (7:4, 11) instead of (as here)

[85] *E.g.*, Pr. 18:4a; 20:5.

[86] It is used in the expression, 'day of disaster', v. 16, and is translated 'incurable' at 15:18; 30:12, 15.

[87] The cryptic Heb. could portray either a partridge which appropriates another's brood (RSV) or clutch (NEB, NIV), or one that fails to hatch its eggs (that 'sitteth on eggs, and hatcheth them not', AV). As against various explanations of the former alternative in terms of folklore, G. S. Cansdale finds that of the AV the most plausible, simply in consequence of the prevalence of nest-robbing, since these eggs are much in demand. He quotes an expedition leader who was brought 800 partridge eggs in one spring (*Animals of Bible Lands* (Paternoster, 1970), pp. 166–167).

[88] Ps. 69:9; Jn. 2:17, AV.

the Lord's *glorious throne* (12). Here too he makes us see the *self-inflicted* plight and self-chosen epitaph of a generation that would rather die of thirst than turn back to the spring (13, *cf.* 2:13).

But the personal cry of verses 14–18 reveals him more intimately: as a preacher smitten by his own message (14); as a prophet without honour (15);[89] and as a bearer of news for which he had no relish (16). Here is the costly inside story of true prophecy, as defined in 2 Pet. 1:21 (NIV): 'For prophecy never had its origin in the will of man, but men spoke from God as they were carried along [even, we learn, under protest] by the Holy Spirit.'

At the end of his prayer (17–18) Jeramiah recalls the warning he received at his commissioning ('Do not be dismayed by them, lest I dismay you before them' (1:17) – for *dismay* is the word he now dwells on, not only in verse 18 but also where verse 17 has *terror* in our versions. On his call for retribution, see the comment on 11:20; but we should not miss the note of 'fear and trembling' (*cf.* 1 Cor. 2:3) which was the cost of his outspokenness. It silently rebukes the blandness of the safe preacher.

A test case for Judah: the Lord's day
17:19–27

The basic reason for this urgent call was the fact that sabbath-keeping was explicitly a badge of loyalty, a sign of the covenant with the Lord (Ex. 31:12–17). It was a good criterion. A people's or a person's reaction to the gift of a day to be set apart for God was a fair indicator of their spiritual temperature; and it still is.

Amos, for example, had portrayed his money-mad contemporaries fuming at the sabbath's interruption of business,

> saying, 'When will the new moon be over,
>   that we may sell grain?
> And the sabbath,
>   that we may offer wheat for sale,
>   … and deal deceitfully with false balances?'
>   (Amos 8:5)

---

[89] See the comment introducing 'Judgment from the north' (4:5 – 6:26), p. 38.

And Nehemiah throws light on the banning of *burdens* on this day, which dominates our passage, by showing the sabbath streets of Jerusalem thronged with shoppers and the paraphernalia of trade: 'In those days I saw in Judah men treading wine presses on the sabbath, and bringing in heaps of grain and loading them on asses; and also wine, grapes, figs, and all kinds of burdens ...' (Ne. 13:15). The sheer scale of it showed how quickly the sabbath could be swamped and lost.

With our human genius for getting things wrong, however, we find the legalists of our Lord's day missing the point and spirit of this prohibition, in the case of the healed man who was told to pick up his mat and walk, on the sabbath[90] – hardly for trade! – just as they missed all our Lord's object-lessons on the subject. For ourselves we can note from these passages the perverse extremes (that of Jeremiah's generation on the one hand, and of Christ's on the other), either of which can ruin the Lord's day: whether by flooding it with the mundane or by freezing it with the forbidden.

The glowing promises in verses 24ff. – of kings in state, and pilgrims flocking with their offerings[91] – may seem out of proportion to the modest prohibition against moving goods on the sabbath. But the positive command to *keep the sabbath day holy* (22) leaves room for the breadth and depth of piety, and is best unfolded in another passage:

> If you turn back your foot from the sabbath
>> from doing your pleasure on my holy day,
> and call the sabbath a delight
>> and the holy day of the Lord honourable ...,
> then you shall take delight in the Lord,
>> and I will make you ride upon the heights of the earth ...
>
> (Is. 58:13–14)

---

[90] Jn. 5:10.

[91] The catalogue of ritual offerings in v. 26 answers any doubt of Jeremiah's attitude to sacrificial worship. His scathing words in 7:22 were an indictment not of the system but of its abuse.

Two parables from pottery, and a violent response   18:1 – 20:18

The setting for these chapters is probably the early years of the reign of Jehoiakim (609–598), with Babylon still a distant threat, but a new regime at home, hostile to Jeremiah and to all that King Josiah had stood for. The parable of chapter 18, where the potter's vessel is still in the making, appeals for national conversion; but chapter 19 shows the vessel hardened beyond changing, fit only to be smashed; whereupon in chapter 20 Jeremiah is flogged and put in the pillory for preaching such a message.

The potter and the clay   18:1–12

The potter at work is one of God's favourite pictures of himself, from Genesis 2:7 onwards.[92] Mostly it puts us firmly in our place, as the clay which has no right to cavil at the craftsman[93] – though we can appeal strongly to his love for what he fashions.[94]

Here, however, the lesson is all about *re*making, for better or worse. We see the potter in his sensitivity to his material, with all its flaws and possibilities. This craftsman is no plodding amateur: his touch has the boldness and resource of the true artist, and we can extrapolate from the immediate setting of the parable, to reflect on God's masterly remaking of a Simon Peter, a Saul of Tarsus, a Ruth, a Matthew, and on the implications for ourselves of so sure a touch and so creative an approach. But its primary message is on a broader scale (*concerning a nation or a kingdom*, 7, 9) and on a sharper issue, for it concentrates on the moment when the human potter was seen to alter his design. That readiness to change – not capricious but self-consistent – corresponds to God's own freedom to revise either his threats (7–8) or his promises (9–10). So every situation becomes an open one: every threat a challenge to repent and see it cancelled; every promise a call to persevere to its fulfilment.

This is a statement of first-class importance for our understanding of all prophecy, removing it entirely from the realm of fatalism.

---

[92] The expression, '[he] formed man', uses the verb of which 'potter' is the participle.
[93] *Cf.* Is. 29:16; 45:9; Rom. 9:20–21.
[94] *Cf.* Ps. 119:73; Is. 64:8.

However stark the prediction (except where God has expressly declared it irreversible[95]), it is always open to revision, whether it is such a threat as Jonah's 'Yet forty days, and Nineveh shall be overthrown!',[96] or such a promise as God's word 'for ever' to the house of Eli, which was revoked with his 'but now ...'[97]

The lesson was not left in the general terms of verses 7–10, but applied with the sharp thrust, *Now, therefore*, of verse 11 – only to receive the bluntest of refusals (12).

A perfidious people   18:13–17

When we ruefully observe the loyalty of entire nations to their man-made religions, in contrast to the drift of 'Christian' countries from the true faith, we are not the first to be amazed. What this divine lament does not allow for a moment, however, is any softening of the charge that the rival gods are false, or any excuse for turning to them (15). It is not only *a very horrible thing* (13), as any betrayal must be: it is as unnatural as to forsake what has never failed –

> Does the snow of Lebanon
>   ever vanish from its rocky slopes?
> Do its cool waters from distant sources
>   ever cease to flow?
>
>   (14, NIV)

– and as perverse as to turn from a known road to a maze of byways (15).

These themes have been enlarged on elsewhere with telling effect (*e.g.*, 2:10–13; 6:16), but there is now a further sting in verse 17 with its evocative allusion to 'the east wind', in which a well-known victory psalm had exulted:

> By the east wind thou didst shatter
>   the ships of Tarshish.[98]

Now the Lord himself will be like such a wind, not to save his people but to scatter them.

---

[95] See, *e.g.*, 7:16; 14:11.
[96] Jon. 3:4, 10.
[97] 1 Sa. 2:30.
[98] Ps. 48:7.

The prophet under threat   18:18–23

Verse 18 is famous for the saying it quotes about three kinds of religious expert (*cf.* the similar Ezk. 7:26). From the priest one would seek a ruling on a point of ritual law (*cf.* Hag. 2:11ff.); from the sage, practical or political advice (*cf.* 2 Sa. 16:23; Is. 19:11); and from the prophet a direct word from the Lord (*e.g.*, Je. 37:17). At first sight the plot to silence Jeremiah runs clean counter to the saying which is quoted to support it; but NEB's paraphrase suggests the reasoning behind it: '... There will still be priests to guide us, still wise men to advise, still prophets to proclaim the word.' In other words, 'There are plenty of fish in the sea: we can do without this one!'[99]

Characteristically, Jeremiah pours out his heart in yet another of the anguished protests which punctuate these chapters and illuminate his story. His wound would have hurt less had he cared less and, paradoxically, prayed less for his people; but the violent swing from love to hate shows how near the surface are the unruly instincts of the best of us. Admittedly, invective has its own momentum and its own conventions (as the cursing passage of 20:14ff. will show), and the prayer of verse 23 against forgiveness needs to be read in Old Testament terms, of punishment in this world rather than the next, and of judicial sentencing.[100] Yet granted all this, the gulf between praying down famine on even the adversaries' children (to go no further into vv. 21–22) and praying down forgiveness on one's tormentors, is the gulf between the resentful 'lamb led to the slaughter' (as Jeremiah described himself, 11:19) and the uncomplaining Lamb of God.[101]

A vessel for destruction   19:1–15

If there is nothing so workable as a clay pot in the making, there is nothing so unalterable as the finished article. If it is wrong by then, that is that.

This acted sequel to Jeremiah's visit to the potter's house and to the rejection of his parable (18:1–12) took place at a doubly

---

[99] Je. 2:8; 5:31; 23:9ff.; 26:7ff.; 28:1ff., are enough to confirm how right they were, in their own terms.

[100] See on 11:20, p. 60.

[101] Is. 53:7; 1 Pet. 2:22–24.

well-chosen spot: at the gate of Broken Pottery, the rubbish gate, that led into the sinister vale of Hinnom. For details of this place, see the comments on 7:27–34. Here we may add two things: first about verse 5, then about verse 9.

The offering of children to Baal (5), under his title of King,[102] has sometimes been represented as a mere dedication rite, passing the child harmlessly over a flame towards the idol. But while one expression, 'to pass over to Molech',[103] could suggest as little as this on its own, our verse 5 and 7:31 leave no doubt that these were actual burnt-offerings, although not burnt alive.[104]

On verse 9 it is enough to refer to the eyewitness account in Lamentations 4:10, together with the rest of that terrible chapter.

At this point (10) Jeremiah was to make his oracle unforgettable (and irreversible, as an acted word from the Lord), by smashing the clay pot as something that was now past remaking.[105] Then, with great courage, he made his way to the stronghold of his enemies, the temple court, with the dire results that will occupy the next chapter.

Jeremiah's arrest and ordeal   20:1–6

So threats have turned to action, introducing Jeremiah to the long sequence of physical sufferings that awaited him. To us, the stocks (more accurately, the pillory) may sound chiefly humiliating, but the Hebrew word is formed from the verb to twist, implying that this 'twist-frame' clamped the victim in a position that would become increasingly distressing.[106] Jeremiah, incidentally, was not the first prophet to be given this treatment: see 2 Chronicles 16:10.

The stern words against Pashhur[107] in verses 4–6 were not

---

[102] Melech or Milcom, derisively pronounced as Molech, to rhyme with *bosheth*, 'shame'.

[103] *E.g.*, 32:35, *etc.*, where AV's explanatory italics, *the fire*, are its addition.

[104] *Cf.* Ezk. 16:20–21, '... these you sacrificed to them to be devoured ... you slaughtered my children and delivered them up ...'

[105] On his additional words about Topheth as a mass grave, see the closing comments on ch. 7.

[106] 29:26 adds 'and collar' to 'the stocks'. A different word for 'stocks' is used in Job 13:27; 33:11; not based on the word for twisting.

[107] 'Son of Immer', v. 1, probably denotes the priestly duty-division to which he belonged, since Immer was the founding father of the sixteenth group (1 Ch. 24:14) set up by David. The Pashhur-ben-Malchiah of the next chapter (21:1) may have been a member of group five, founded by the Malchijah of 1 Ch. 24:9.

Jeremiah's own, unlike his prayers against his enemies, but a divine oracle, in keeping with God's concern to vindicate his word. We have already seen at 6:25 that *Terror on every side* (*Magor Missabib*) is a phrase that echoes through this book. To become a living, abject picture of it was no more than justice on one who had tried to break a brave man's spirit and had shown the cheap courage of defying the invisible God. The priest of Bethel, 150 years earlier, had been as sharply sentenced when he tried to silence Amos;[108] and certain false prophets would be given a divine death-sentence later in Jeremiah's ministry.[109] Others, of course, would oppose the truth with impunity; but these exemplary sentences show what God thought of them, and (we must add) what he thinks of their successors, whom we meet in, *e.g.*, 2 Timothy 4:3–4; Galatians 1:6–9.

From protest to praise 20:7–13

If ever one's morale as a servant of God touches rock-bottom, we may reflect that Jeremiah has been there before, and has survived. Notice his deep doubts of his message (7a), the wounds to his self-esteem (7b – is there anything more deadly than ridicule?), the feeling that he is only shouting 'Wolf! Wolf!' (8), and perhaps worst of all, the knowledge that his closest friends have turned against him (10).

Through it all, though, he feels that he is wrestling, not simply with himself or with them, but with God (for the whole passage is a prayer, not a soliloquy). The opening cry, *Thou hast deceived me*, carries the dreadful fear that he has earned the penalty of the false prophet: to be trapped in one's falsehood and used as a decoy to lure himself and others to ruin.[110] On the other hand, he knows that the fiery message he cannot contain (9) is *the word of the Lord*, whatever people say (8b), and that the Lord does know his honest heart (12a).[111] So he emerges from his doubts (11–12)[112] – and surely in verse 13 we have his very words as he emerges also from his overnight confinement (*the needy* is in the singular).

---

[108] Am. 7:10–17.

[109] *I.e.*, Hananiah, 28:16–17; Ahab and Zedekiah, 29:21–23.

[110] *Cf.* 1 Ki. 22:19–23; Ezk. 14:7–10.

[111] But it is significant that when the New Testament discusses our heart-searchings it points us to a higher touchstone than sincerity. It wants evidence of love. See 1 Jn. 3:19–21, with its opening words which refer back to its v. 18.

[112] On his plea for vengeance, see again on 11:20.

Jeremiah curses his day   20:14–18

Like Job, plunging to the depths after each high point of faith,[113] Jeremiah suffers a desolating reaction which brings now the long series of his protests and laments to a close. After this, as though by now he is God's metal fully tempered (*cf.* 15:20), he goes on to his worst ordeals with never a hesitation or a word of doubt.

Quite apart from the insight he gives us into his depression (with nothing argumentative or theological to shape the passage: only a wild cry of pain), he may give us by his very extravagance a clue to some other extremes of invective in Scripture. For even if (which is unlikely) he genuinely wished a particular day of the year to become one of ill omen (14), he certainly could not have seriously consigned his father's friend to misery and death for not perpetrating a double murder (15–17)!

What these curses convey, therefore, is a state of mind, not a prosaic plea. The heightened language is not there to be analysed: it is there to bowl us over. Together with other tortured cries from him and his fellow sufferers, these raw wounds in Scripture remain lest we forget the sharpness of the age-long struggle, or the frailty of the finest overcomers.

[113] *E.g.*, Jb. 2:10 with 3:1ff.; 14:13ff. with 18ff.; 19:25ff. with 21:1ff.

PART TWO: Jeremiah 21 – 45
From Josiah's successors to the captivity
'...What will happen when the wood is dry?'

For the sequence of events in the quarter-century that followed the death of King Josiah in 609 BC, see the Introduction on 'The life and times of Jeremiah', especially pp. 18ff. But the book of Jeremiah is prophecy, not chronicle, therefore many of the following chapters move freely back and forth within these final years, as their date-lines show. This is particularly true of the next six.

Leaves from the last years of Judah
21:1 – 26:24

One possible explanation of the time-leaps here is the fact that Jeremiah made many additions to his writings when he replaced the scroll destroyed by King Jehoiakim (36:32). If some of these addenda were written on whatever came to hand in those unsettled years, the chapters as we have them could still be in the order in which the unedited pile of documents confronted the faithful Baruch after Jeremiah's death. In that case they may add their involuntary witness to the vicissitudes that they survived, and to their editor's reluctance to impose his own pattern on them.

Less speculatively, the fact that Jeremiah's oracles are generally arranged by subject rather than by chronology may point here to a deliberate placing, for a start, of chapters 20 and 21 side by side as a prophecy and its fulfilment; for we see first Babylon as a distant threat (20:4–6), and now Babylon at the gates (21:4).[1] The ensuing chapters, too, may be placed here to give the reader a swift view of the useless kings (ch. 22; 24:8–10) and prophets (23:9–40) of Judah's last two decades, while offering in 23:1–8 and 24:4–7 two distinct gleams of hope. The fact, however, that meanwhile judgment must precede this renewal, is brought out by prediction and preaching in chapters 25 and 26.

Surrender or perish!   21:1–14

This episode, c.588, transports us suddenly to the final siege of Jerusalem, some twenty years after the events of chapter 20. For its context, we must wait for chapters 32, 34, 37 – 39.

It was typical of the vacillating King Zedekiah to turn to Jeremiah in a crisis, but to lack the courage or integrity to act on his advice.[2] He had been installed as puppet-king in Jerusalem by Nebuchadrezzar, after the previous king and the cream of the population had been carried off to Babylon in 597. He had sworn fealty to his overlord in the name of God (2 Ch. 36:13), but broke his oath as soon as he felt confident of support from Egypt. (God's disgust at such treachery can be seen in Ezk. 17:15: 'Will he succeed? Can a man escape who does such things?') So, in the ninth year of his reign, the Babylonian army has arrived for the kill.

---

[1] A subsidiary factor in this grouping may have been the catchword provided by the name Pashhur, borne by the two men whose contrasting approaches to Jeremiah underline the fact that the march of events was already confirming his predictions.

[2] Cf. the similar deputation a little later, during a brief lifting of the siege (37:3–10); then his secret interviews at 37:16–21; 38:14–26.

Of the two delegates who were sent with their humble request, the Pashhur of verse 1 was no friendlier to Jeremiah than his namesake of the previous chapter, for he would later be one of the group who committed him to the miry dungeon (38:1, 6). Nor was his fellow envoy Zephaniah at all a reassuring figure, since he was now the officer responsible for putting 'mad' prophets like Jeremiah in the stocks (29:25–27), and had indeed held this threat over him a few years before (29:29).

Through such a pair of emissaries, then, and to such a traitor-king, it was as dangerous as it was a duty to send back a message of unsparing truth. It could hardly have been more strongly put. If the preview of events was merciless (3–7), the call to surrender, addressed to the citizens over the king's head (8–10) was shattering.[3] After that, the demand to the royal house for energetic social justice (11, 12a, *cf.* Ps. 101:8), and the warning that in default of this God would be a consuming fire (12b–14), confirmed the moral basis for it all – a basis that was even wider and deeper than the particular oath and covenant that the king had broken.

A sad parade of kings   22:1–30

Brought together in one passage, these contemporary comments from God on each successor to King Josiah in turn drive home to us the necessity – and the miracle – of the perfect King to come.

King and kingdom in the balance   22:1–9

The thrust of this, and the form of its opening words (2–3a), are close enough to the message sent back to King Zedekiah to suggest at first sight that we are still dealing with the same man. But it seems more likely that this paragraph was a much earlier message, to another king, since there is still time for the house of David to recover strongly (*riding in chariots and on horses, they, and their servants, and their people*, 4), whereas in 21:12–14 the only options left to the final king are between degrees of punishment.

---

[3] The disloyalty of such a call was apparent rather than real, since Judah was in rebellion against her overlord, whose authority God endorsed (ch. 27). A surrender, whatever its motives, would be an act of due submission. Jeremiah himself did not take this course, though he was accused of attempting it (37:11–15), but he continued to preach it and was severely punished for doing so (38:2, 3, 6).

Here, then, we may well be at that turning-point for Judah when the untimely death of King Josiah in 609 left all his reforms open to challenge, and his throne to be occupied by men of a different stamp. At this point the spiritual choice is still open, in the words, *For if you will...* (4) *But if you will not...*(5); but the contrast between verses 3 and 17 shows what King Jehoiakim thought of it, and what in consequence he became. His eleven-year reign, however, was briefly preceded by that of his younger brother, the subject of the next oracle.

The hapless King Shallum   22:10–12

Shallum, better known as Jehoahaz,[4] was the people's choice, passing over his elder brother Jehoiakim. This may have been for personal or political reasons (was Shallum the better patriot, as Pharaoh Neco evidently judged?) but not for any leanings towards his father's faith. His three-months' reign was enough to dispose of that idea (2 Ki. 23:32). Yet there is real compassion for him, cut off at only twenty-three years of age from his taste of kingship and from the land he obviously loved.

> *Weep not for him who is dead...*
> *but weep bitterly for him who goes away* (10)

– for there is more than just the poetic paradox of having tears for the living rather than the dead: it is the feeling that Josiah had fought his fight and all-but finished his course, while this young man would have no achievements to look back on, nor goals to live for.

(The career of Joseph, another deportee to Egypt, or the prison years of Paul, give the potential answer to these negatives, where faith is present!)

Jehoiakim the tyrant   22:13–19

Ruthlessness, even in a great enterprise, is never without guilt; but

---

[4] Jehoahaz ('Yahweh holds') was his throne-name, and Shallum evidently his personal name. Well chosen throne-names could be politically reassuring; hence even foreign overlords made use of them. Pharaoh Neco renamed Eliakim Jehoiakim (2 Ki. 23:34), as a gesture towards Yahweh; and Nebuchadrezzar called Mattaniah ('gift of Yahweh') Zedekiah ('righteousness of Yahweh'), 2 Ki. 24:17. In any case, a renaming served to emphasize the overlord's dominance over his puppet.

in aid of self-aggrandizement it is beyond excuse. This man, who gave his mind to trivialities at a time of crisis, and who saw his subjects only as exploitable, was a vulture at law and a peacock at home. Perhaps because royal vultures were nothing new, the first stricture here in on his fine feathers: that gorgeous and totally irrelevant palace.

> *Do you think you are a king*
> *because you compete in cedar?* (15).

But the palace was unpaid-for (13), and beneath the king's panache there was only a small and cruel mind:

> *But you have eyes and heart*
> *only for your dishonest gain,*
> *for shedding innocent blood,*
> *and for practising oppression and violence* (17).

The motto, 'Live so as to be missed', was not for him: rather, the more flattering 'Live so as to be feared' – but his ignominious end (18–19) shows what is left when the fear is past. He died in fetters, unlamented, about to be deported to Babylon (2 Ch. 36:6). According to Josephus (*Antiquities*, X.vi.3) it was Nebuchadrezzar who had his body 'thrown before the walls, without any burial'.

In contrast to this, we can be grateful for the retrospect on his father:

(Josiah the just   22:15b–16)

So much is told us of Josiah's strenuous reforms,[5] that we may think of him too much as a stickler for pure worship, too little as a shepherd of his flock. Here the balance is restored, in terms which anticipate our Lord's own dedication to his calling: 'My food is to do the will of him who sent me...' (Jn. 4:34).

> *Did not your father eat and drink*
> *and do justice and righteousness?* (15b).

If we want to follow the three themes of verse 16 further (care for the needy; the gift of well-being; true knowledge of God), they are glowingly described in Isaiah 58:6–9a, in terms that are not confined to kings.

[5] 2 Ki. 22 – 23; 2 Ch. 34 – 35.

A friendless kingdom   22:20–23

There is a double clue to the talk of Lebanon here (20, 23): first, a reminder of the king's frivolous obsession with his cedar wood (14, 15, 23), Lebanon's famous product; but secondly, a return to the warning of verses 6–7,

> You are as Gilead to me,
>   as the summit of Lebanon,
> yet surely I will make you a desert...

– for Lebanon with its glorious forests was the very picture of beauty and prosperity, as was Bashan (20) with its rich pastures. As for Abarim (20), this was the mountain range in the south-east from which Moses had viewed the promised land.[6] All of these were names rich in history or in natural resource; but neither history nor nature, nor again, the inconstant allies spoken of as *your lovers* (Egypt above all) would avail against the wind of judgment (22) – that 'hot wind from the bare heights in the desert...not to winnow or cleanse, a wind too full for this' (*cf*. 4:11–13).

The epitaph on Judah in verse 21 could be that of many a nation, church or individual:

> *I spoke to you in your prosperity,*
>   *but you said, 'I will not listen.'*

Happy if we can yet add the postscript from Psalm 119:67,

> Before I was afflicted I went astray;
>   but now I keep thy word.

Coniah[7] the exile   22:24–30

Like his uncle Jehoahaz (Shallum, 11), this young man of eighteen was king for only three months, before the wrath of Babylon descended on him for his father's rebellion. That father was Jehoiakim, who had lived long enough to corrupt him (2 Ki. 24:9) and to jeopardise his country (2 Ki. 24:1), but who died in time to escape the full consequence.

We have already seen that nothing could now alter God's decision to end the kingdom of Judah;[8] and because a king even in exile may

---

[6] Dt. 32:49; 34:1.

[7] Better known as Jeconiah or Jehoiachin.

[8] *E.g.*, 14:11–12; 15:1; 19:10–11.

remain a focus of wild hopes, God uses here the most violent metaphors (24–28) and then the plainest speaking (30) to refute them. Yet the tone is tragic rather than dismissive, as the whole land – perhaps the whole world[9] – is called to ponder what is happening. The old translation of verse 29 (AV) is uniquely impressive – 'O earth, earth, earth, hear the word of the Lord' – and while the first hearers were doubtless meant to take this word to heart chiefly in its narrower sense (*O land...*), we do well to give it its full scope. The helpless leadership and bitter plight of this small country which had lost its soul, is an object-lesson for all time and all nations: not least for those to whom the words of verse 21 (quoted earlier) apply.

In God's mercy, nevertheless, there was to be a tempering of the wind to that shorn lamb Coniah/Jehoiachin. He was indeed deported (and his name can still be read on a Babylonian list of foreign prisoners and their rations of oil and barley[10]), but eventually he was released and given hospitality at the palace in Babylon (2 Ki. 25:27–30). Furthermore, although he was reckoned *childless* (30) in the sense that none of his direct descendants succeeded him as king, yet another branch of David's family was counted as his legal succession, bringing his name (along with others that are no less flawed) into the genealogy of Christ (Mt. 1:12).

A people misruled and mistaught   23:1–40

Shepherds false and true   23:1–4

For all the influence that a king could have, the detailed handling of affairs naturally belonged to his subordinates, on whose honesty and diligence, or on the opposite of these things, hung the weal or woe – even the livelihood – of the ordinary citizen. These men, and the king, rather than the religious leaders, are what the Old Testament calls shepherds;[11] and all history shows how strongly such office-bearers, high and low, are tempted to abuse their trust. If this passage brings chapter 22's survey of kings down to Zedekiah's reign

---

[9] In Heb. the same word serves for 'the land' and 'the earth'. *Cf.*, *e.g.*, Gn. 1:1; 2:11–13.

[10] A photograph of this tablet, now in the Berlin Museum, is shown in, *e.g.*, D. J. Wiseman, *Illustrations from Biblical Archaeology* (IVP, 1958), p. 73. Also in *IBD*, 2, p. 738.

[11] See esp. Ezk. 34, which develops the theme of our passage at length.

(see on v.6), it is very fitting that it concentrates on his ruthless officials, to whose tune, pathetically, he danced. 'The king', he once said, 'can do nothing against you' (38:5).

But this very spectacle of bad shepherding makes God all the more determined, if we may put it so, to round up the scattered flock and find good shepherds for it, just as in Isaiah he had promised a regime where not only 'a king will reign in righteousness' but 'princes will rule in justice; each...like a hiding place from the wind,...like streams of water in a dry place'.[12] (Here is a model for all administrators!)

The perfect king   23:5–6

So comes the messianic promise of the *righteous Branch* or 'shoot' of new growth[13] from David's dying dynasty. Among his attributes, that of dealing wisely (5) is revealed in new depth in the light of Isaiah 52:13 ('prosper', RSV), where it introduces the account of the Servant's work of atonement for his people. It was in that richer sense that the words of our verse 6 would come true: *In his days Judah will be saved.*[14]

As for his name, *The Lord is our righteousness* (6), it is perhaps doubly significant, for at one level its meaning is almost identical with that of Zedekiah ('righteousness of the Lord'), creating a pointed contrast to the current king, whose life so desperately belied his name.[15] But in its own right it speaks of one who will not only reflect the righteousness of God but will convey it to his people, making it their own possession.[16] Paul may have had this promise in mind when he spoke of 'Christ Jesus...our righteousness...' (1 Cor. 1:30, *cf.* 2 Cor. 5:21).

---

[12] Is. 32:1–2. The word for 'princes' refers to officials, not to royal sons.

[13] This word, *ṣemaḥ*, 'shoot', recurs at 33:15; Zc. 3:8; 6:12. Other messianic terms with the same emphasis on new life out of apparent death are found at Is. 11:1; 53:2.

[14] *Cf.* Mt. 1:21, 'he will save his people from their sins'.

[15] So this passage may be a cryptic postscript to the series on contemporary kings in the previous chapter.

[16] While the Messiah's names in, *e.g.*, Is. 9:6 imply his deity, this name does not state it, since in 33:15–16 the same name is given to Jerusalem. Rather, it says what God will be to his people ('our righteousness') in and through his promised king.

The greater Exodus   23:7–8

Under the shadow of the Babylonian Exile (an exile already in progress for such as Daniel since 605, and for King Jehoiachin and his leading citizens since 597),[17] God loved to raise his people's eyes to the promised homecoming, as a new and greater Exodus. The event would prove that he had in mind much more than the return of some forty thousand in the days of Cyrus, although that would be wonderful enough as a first instalment. See the comments on 16:14–21, where our present verses have already appeared; and see the fuller prophecies of, *e.g.*, Isaiah 60:19ff.; 65:17ff.

Prophets false and true   23:9–40

There is far more concern here, and far more heartbreak (9), over false preachers than over brutal officials (the 'shepherds' of vv. 1–2) – for without justice a nation suffers, but without truth it sickens. Worse still, these ungodly prophets and priests are not simply useless, failing to give a lead, for by their position their lives and words are a fountain pouring out what others will drink (*cf.* 15c with the 'muddied spring' of Pr. 25:26). By their worldliness they are secularizing the house of God (11), that bastion of holiness; and by their laxity (14), whether practised or preached, they are taking the shame out of sin (especially, it seems, sins of lust, both heterosexual, 14a, and homosexual, 14b; *cf.* Gn. 19:4–5). Even the heresy of the northern prophets is less culpable than the laxity of these southerners (13–14, *cf.* 2:11).

Along with easy views of sin go rosy views of judgment, since (as vv. 16–17 point out) such prophets *speak visions of their own minds*, naturally imagining that God's thoughts must be as enlightened as their own. What else can one think, from such a starting-point?

So in verses 18–22 we reach the heart of the matter: God is speaking of the difference between conjecture and revelation. As an analogy in modern terms we could compare the speculations of journalists over some matter of government which is being decided behind closed doors, with the actual announcement entrusted to a spokesman from the conclave itself. As verse 28b (AV) will exclaim, 'What is the chaff to the wheat?' But the best comment on verse 18 is what is said of the supreme Revealer, who not only *stood in the*

[17] Dn. 1:1; 2 Ki. 24:12–16.

council of the Lord but is eternally 'in the bosom of the Father' (Jn. 1:18, *cf.* Mt. 11:27). Even the terms of our verse, *to perceive* (lit., 'see') *and to hear his word*, are echoed by Christ in John 8:38, 40: 'I speak of what I have *seen* with my Father...; the truth which I *heard* from God'. This precision is as important for us as it was for Jeremiah's generation, for there is always a temptation to listen to rumour rather than revelation, leaving one's theological options apparently open.

Perhaps the most damning comment on the self-appointed prophets, however, besides the mounting absurdity of having no mission, no message and no access to God (21–22),[18] is the fact that they have nothing to say about sin and repentance (22b): only about peace and prosperity (17). Yet this is the very way to miss these goals – a fact which we may still need to learn.

Verses 23–24 give us one of the great sayings about the inescapable presence of God, whose nearness is as penetrating and searching at the farthest reaches of the universe as it is where one is standing now. While Psalm 139 grows lyrical about this, here the tone is as ominous as it is in Amos 9:2–4; for the false prophets are still in mind. Like the rest of us, they manage to forget that their cleverest disguises are in full view of God, who knows the truth about their impressive dreams; who also knows the truth about our human love of the sensational, which distracts the mind from reality as effectively as any heresy (27).

It is in fact the *levity* of these preachers which angers God as much as their lies – that they dare to preach borrowed clichés (30) and airy speculations (*their recklessness*, 32) *in the name of the Lord* (as if, in modern terms, to preface their unbiblical sermons with the formula, 'In the name of the Father, the Son and the Holy Spirit').

So the chapter ends (33–40) with a relentless attack on one of these prophetic clichés, *the burden* (or 'oracle') *of the Lord*. Many of Isaiah's prophecies had some such heading,[19] since this word, *maśśā'*, comes from the verb 'to lift', and could refer to lifting up one's voice or to picking up a burden. These men have made it meaningless, so God not only puts a ban on it but makes a wrathful pun on it, once if not twice. In one reading of verse 33 his retort to

---

[18] 'Council' (*sôḏ*) has the suggestion of an intimate circle of trusted friends. *Cf.* Ps. 25:14, where this word is translated 'friendship', ʀsv; *cf.* 'The Lord confides in ...', ɴɪv; *Cf.* also Am. 3:7, where the Lord opens 'his secret [the same word] to his servants the prophets'.

[19] 'The burden of Babylon ...of Moab ... of Damascus', *etc.* (Is. 13:1; 15:1; 17:1, ᴀv).

the question, *What is the burden of the Lord?* is, 'You are the burden, and I will cast you off.'[20] Finally in verses 39–40 he takes and emphasizes the parent verb of 'burden' in its literal sense, to visualize these men picked up and thrown away in irretrievable disgrace.

Is there something to be learnt from this vehement reaction to the downgrading of God's word?

Good fruit and bad: the exiles and the exempt   24:1–10

The natural reaction to the fate of the captives deported in 597, and to the good fortune of those who were left behind, was to see the former as God's throw-outs, the *bad figs*; and to see the rest as his men of promise, the *good figs* that were worth keeping. But, as ever, God's thoughts and plans were not at all what men imagined. This chapter may be placed here partly to emphasize this very fact, driving home the warnings of the previous chapter against the prophets who fancied that they could guess the mind of God. For the unexpected was the truth. The future lay with the exiles, not with the treacherous regime of Zedekiah and the politicians who manipulated him in Jerusalem or intrigued in Egypt (8). So indeed it turned out.

Notice, however, the heavenly dimension which is paramount in God's reply. While men's thoughts would dwell on politics and patriotism and on the puzzling distribution of suffering, God speaks of having *sent* the exiles to Chaldea (5), and of *regard[ing them] as good* (5), not in view of their merits but of what the New Testament would call his grace – that is, of the good which he planned to do for them (6) and, above all, within them (7).

There is always this dimension for those who are 'called according to his purpose' (Rom. 8:28) – transcending but not preventing the 'tribulation ... distress ... persecution ...' and the rest of Paul's list in Romans 8:35–39. The relation between the two dimensions, human and divine, has never been better put than by Joseph to his brothers in Genesis 50:20: 'As for you, you meant evil against me; but God meant it for good, to bring it about that many people should be kept alive, as they are today.'

---

[20] So, *e.g.*, RSV, NEB, JB, following LXX, Vg. This reading involves no alteration of the Heb. consonants.

A turning-point in history 25:1–38

After the preview given in chapters 21 – 24 of the disastrous years 609–597, in which no fewer than four kings came to the throne after the death of Josiah, we return to the moment when the second of these kings, Jehoiakim, found himself the subject of a new world-ruler, Nebuchadrezzar of Babylon. The year was 605, in which the battle of Carchemish had put an end to Egypt's bid for world-dominion, leaving Babylon supreme. (Egypt's rout is vividly portrayed in 46:2–12.)

So it was a time that raised alarming questions over the rise and fall of empires and the future of one's own people. The prophets of chapter 23 would be full of their latest dreams and their reassuring catchwords. In this atmosphere of speculation God gives Jeremiah a message that starts not with prediction but with preaching (1–7) – for it is on this basis that he goes on to reveal what is immediately in store for Israel and its neighbours far and near: a lifetime, but no more (11), of subservience to Babylon, before that empire in its turn is overthrown (8–14). The chapter then goes on to spell this out by naming these subjected peoples,[21] describing their judgment as a cup of wrath from the hand of God (15–26). But since these kingdoms made up virtually the entire world of the Old Testament, the final verses can go on to speak in more and more sweeping terms, to present finally a picture which transcends these limits, to be fulfilled (as I see it) in the truly universal judgment of the end-time.

We now pick up a few details in the chapter for comment.

Time for judgment 25:1–7

Verses 1 and 3 give us the first precise dates in the book since the mention of Josiah's thirteenth year in 1:2 – underlining the importance of this moment in world history, but also the patience of God in preaching for the past twenty-three years to an already unresponsive people. Verses 4–7 lead inexorably to the 'Therefore' of verse 8.

Enter and exit Babylon 25:8–14

In verse 9 notice the term *Nebuchadrezzar... my servant* (repeated in

[21] This anticipates the detailed prophecies of chs. 46 – 51, which are in fact inserted here in LXX, between our vv. 13 and 15.

27:6). As Cyrus was called 'my shepherd' and the Lord's 'anointed', although he did not know the Lord,[22] so Nebuchadrezzar was to be God's unwitting servant – recalling us again to the great truth about men's 'wicked hands' fulfilling God's 'determinate counsel'.[23]

The *seventy years* of Babylon's ascendancy (11, 12, *cf.* 27:7) turned out to be a round number which God mercifully shortened; for Babylon fell to Cyrus not in 535 but four years earlier, in 539. We can be reminded of the similar mercy promised in Matthew 24:22, and of many an undeserved relenting in God's dealings with us – even with an Ahab (1 Ki. 21:27–29),[24] and classically with the Israel of the Old Testament, towards whom he frequently 'relented according to the abundance of his steadfast love' (Ps. 106:45).

The wine of wrath   25:15–29

The *cup* which dominates this passage is by no means confined to it:[25] Gethsemane has made it poignant for us by our Lord's acceptance of it in our place.[26] But in its familiar reference to nations and their downfall, its picture of judgment in the form of drunken stupor and collapse is all too recognizable in the collective madness that can take hold of a people to destroy it from within, by godless infatuations and perversions. The spectacle of verses 16 and 27 is no exaggeration in such a case.

(On a point of detail: 'Babylon' in v.26 is written in cipher: not in its Heb. form, 'Babel', but as *šešak*, by changing the three consonants of Babel (the 2nd, 2nd and 12th in the alphabet) to š, š, ḵ, the 2nd, 2nd and 12th from the alphabet's end. The same method is used at 51:1 (for Chaldea) and 51:41 (for Babel). In the text as it stands, where Babylon and Chaldea are named openly and often, it conceals nothing; but it gives a glimpse into the precautions which people evidently had to take at times in conversation or correspondence.)

Notice finally, in this section, the principle in verse 29 that judgment must 'begin with the household of God': *cf.* 1 Peter 4:17; Amos 3:2.

---

[22] Is. 44:28; 45:1, 5.

[23] Acts 2:23, AV, *cf.* Gn. 50:20; Rom. 9:17.

[24] And potentially – need we doubt? – with his son, should he too repent.

[25] See esp. Pss. 60:3; 75:8; Is. 51:17, 22; Rev. 16:19.

[26] *Cf.* Lk. 22:41–42; Jn. 18:11.

The lion's roar   25:30–38

While the picture of verses 15–29 emphasizes the bemusing and self-acting process of judgment, the final paragraphs redress the balance with the personal energy of the Lord, as a lion[27] about to ravage the *peaceful folds* (37) and the *lords of the flock* (34, 35, 36): in other words, to judge a world which thinks itself secure, and the high and mighty who think themselves the shepherds of their people.[28] Man proposes; God disposes.

A courageous sermon and its sequel   26:1–24

The sermon   26:1–6

A longer account or a longer version of this sermon, but without the furore that now followed it, appears in chapter 7, undated; so it is an open question whether it was preached on two occasions or only one.[29] But this date, early in the reign of Jehoiakim (609–598), is significant, for everything was now in flux. Little more than three months had seen King Josiah killed in battle, his successor deported to Egypt, and this third king, a man of no scruples, imposed on the country.[30] At such a moment, to give strong warnings of potentially worse things in store was to take one's life in one's hands, especially when these warnings touched the temple and the holy city, popularly thought to be inviolable. Instead, *If you will not listen to me* (the Lord) ... *then I will make this house like Shiloh,*[31] *and I will make this city a curse for all the nations of the earth* (4, 6). No matter that all this was conditional: even a rumour of a word against the temple would still be enough, half a millennium later, to put a man's life at risk.[32]

The sequel   26:7–19

What now followed is a striking example of the fallibility of experts

---

[27] *Cf.* Am. 1:2; 3:4, 8, 12.
[28] *Cf.* 23:1–4, and comments there. *Cf.*, in a different sense, 1 Pet. 5:1–4.
[29] See the introductory comments to 7:1 – 8:3.
[30] See ch. 22 and the comments there.
[31] *Cf.* 7:12; Ps. 78:60.
[32] Mt. 26:59–62; Acts 6:12–14; 21:28ff.

when their prejudices are aroused. Happily the priests and prophets had to bring their case before a cross-section of administrators and other citizens, who had no special axe to grind. But the decisive factor was the informed reasoning of the elders (17): that is, of respected laymen who had made their own study of the Scriptures. (Without this broad base of the well-taught in the word of God, a church is too much at the mercy of its professionals!)

The precedent they cited can be found in Micah 3:12 and in the story of Isaiah 37: a sequence of events that perfectly illustrates the wisdom of listening to unwelcome truth, just as the events of 587 BC and of AD 70 show the folly of the more instinctive reaction.

A postscript   26:20–24

These verses, rounding off the chapter rather than the elders' speech (for the murder of Uriah after his vain escape to Egypt is unlikely to have taken place as early in the new reign as this; see v.1), show what kind of tyrant had come to power, and what courage was needed in a prophet. They also remind the reader that God's decisions are matters for his wisdom, not ours. Uriah was to glorify God by martyrdom; Jeremiah still had many years of speaking and suffering to fulfil. Meanwhile these dangerous days revealed another man of courage in Ahikam (24), one of a faithful family[33] and of a small number of others who would come forward when they were most needed and most at risk.

---

[33] Josiah had sent Ahikam, with four others, to consult the prophetess Huldah over the new-found book of the law (2 Ki. 22:12). His brother, Gemariah, dared to put a room at Baruch's disposal for the public reading of Jeremiah's scroll, and to protest against the king's burning of the document (36:10, 25). Ahikam's son Gedaliah took Jeremiah under his wing after the fall of Jerusalem (39:14).

Babylon in God's plan   27:1 – 29:32

Accept the conqueror's yoke!   27:1 – 28:17

Jeremiah and the conspirators   *27:1–11*

Events that look like total disaster and humiliation may wear a very different aspect with the benefit of hindsight; how much more with the wisdom of heaven! Jeremiah's disturbing gifts of thongs and yoke-bars[34] to the visiting diplomats of verse 3 (whose talk with King Zedekiah[35] will hardly have been confined to the weather) must have seemed as insulting and defeatist as they appeared to Jeremiah's own people. Yet chapters 46 – 51 will show how ripe for judgment were these neighbours, and what mercy lay beyond the judgment for many of them (as our v.7 already hints). Above all, this sign and oracle proclaimed the world-wide sovereignty of *the Lord of hosts, the God of Israel* (4), to whom even the greatest power on earth is unwittingly *my servant* (6).[36]

Jeremiah confronts the false prophets   *27:12 – 28:17*

The impact of all this on Jeremiah's own people was reinforced by a personal appeal to the king (27:12–15), by a public speech (16) and by the spectacle of the prophet himself wearing the ominous yoke (27:2; 28:10). Against this, his fellow prophets fought with the familiar weapons of religious conflict: with sweeping assertions on emotive issues, and finally the resort to intimidation.[37] The emotive issues were the hopes centred on the temple vessels[38] (for people have always focused more passionately on holy objects than on appeals for holy living) and on a swift reunion with the exiles (28:4).

---

[34] The Heb. of v.3 reads 'Send them ...', not 'Send word ...' A sign added potency to a prophet's words.

[35] The MT has 'Jehoiakim' in v.1, but 28:1 shows that Zedekiah was the king in question. A few Heb. mss and Syr. support the reading 'Zedekiah' at 27:1.

[36] See also 25:9, and comment.

[37] On the latter, see below, on 29:24–32.

[38] 27:16ff.; 28:3.

It was easy to undercut Jeremiah's talk of seventy years' captivity[39] and his call to pray against a further deportation (27:18–22), with an airy pledge of liberation in a mere two years (28:3, 11) – and to dramatize it by ripping off the offending yoke (28:10).

Jeremiah's personal reaction to all this is a model. His generous *Amen! May the Lord do so* ... (28:6) came, we may believe, from the heart, as his earlier wrestlings with God suggest ('I have not pressed thee to send evil, nor have I desired the day of disaster, thou knowest ...'[40]). At the same time he knew that all the evidence was against an easy answer – not only from what he himself had learnt about such answers (23:16–17), but from his predecessors' preaching (28:8). A further exemplary reaction was his restraint in simply walking away when Hananiah broke off his symbolic yoke (28:11), and in replying only when a word was given him from the Lord (12).[41] Even Paul could have joined us here in learning something from him! (Acts 23:1–5).

But God's word, when it came, was unsparing: first in the general truth of 28:13 that we only add to our chastening when we resist it – exchanging wood for iron. But secondly, the personal word to Hananiah (28:15–17) agrees with a major burden of these chapters: the literally deadly sin (16b) of false prophecy. What we might describe as wishful and unorthodox teaching, God more briefly calls *a lie* (15) and *rebellion* (16). He condemns it not only as offending against truth and against his authority, but as doing a fatal disservice to the hearers: *you have made this people* trust *in a lie* (15).

Paul, in a more characteristic vein than his outburst above, can provide a constructive footnote to the moral of this story. 'I testify to you this day that I am innocent of the blood of all of you, for I did not shrink from declaring to you the whole counsel of God' (Acts 20:26–27).

The letter to the captives   29:1–32

This is still part of the battle that Jeremiah had to fight against the

---

[39] 25:11; 29:10.

[40] 17:16.

[41] While the Heb. of v.12 has simply 'after', not 'Sometime after' (rsv) or 'Shortly after' (niv), the command to 'Go, tell Hananiah...' confirms that there was an interval between the two encounters. For another instance see 42:4, 7.

liberation preachers of his day – for among the captives as well as in Jerusalem there were prophets stirring up false hopes of almost instant freedom, as verses 15ff. will show.

'Seek the welfare of the city ...' 29:1–9

Even the New Testament, with its instructions to overcome evil with good and to 'adorn the doctrine of God' by 'perfect courtesy toward all men',[42] hardly outstrips the boldness of this teaching. Notice the starting-point, that God has *sent* these exiles to Babylon (4, reiterated in 7). At the very least, then, they should accept the situation;[43] but God has little use for grudging attitudes. What emerges in the call to them in verses 5–7 is gloriously positive: a liberation from the paralysing sullenness of inertia and self-pity, into doing, for a start, what comes to hand and makes for growth, but above all what makes for peace.[44] To set themselves something to live for, and something to *give* their captors, through their enterprise (*seek* ...) and their intercession (*pray* ...), was incidentally the surest way – and still is – to the givers' own enrichment, as verse 7b points out. All this (God warns them, 8–9) could be let slip in a preoccupation with idle dreams and propaganda.

'A future and a hope' 29:10–14

With God there is nothing skimped or superficial. The two-year exile promised by the false prophets (28:3, 11) would have been a cruelly pointless march and countermarch; but in a span of seventy years there was a role for Babylon (10a) on the world stage; there were great deeds and visions for such as Daniel to bequeath to us; and there was time for Israel's heart-searching and for the kind of praying that we find in, *e.g.*, Isaiah 63:7 – 64:12. Those who returned would be, for all their faults, pioneers zealous for the purity of Israel; but our verses 12–13 look for a personal and heart-whole openness to God which neither Israel nor the church has often

[42] Rom. 12:21; Tit. 2:10; 3:2, *cf.* 1 Pet. 2:18.

[43] *Cf.* Rom. 13:2, 'Therefore he who resists the authorities resists what God has appointed'.

[44] By translating *šālôm* (7) as 'welfare' (RSV, NEB) or as 'peace and prosperity' (NIV), the modern versions acknowledge the rich content of this word.

shown. God's 'plans for *šālôm*...',[45] *to give you a future and a hope* (11) went deeper and further, as they still do, than prosperity; and the call of verse 13 to seek and find is as fresh as its promise is inexhaustible.[46]

Beware of false prophets   29:15–23

In Babylon it was tempting for the first main wave of exiles to pin their hopes on the fact that, after all, Jerusalem was still intact, still inhabited, and possessed of the temple and a Davidic king. In Babylon too, as at home, there were prophets (15) stirring up these sentiments.

So the truth about the homeland and the truth about these prophets had to be told. In the phrase, *vile figs which are so bad they cannot be eaten* (17), Jeremiah was quoting from the vision God had given him in chapter 24 (see above, p. 93) of the spineless King Zedekiah, his scheming politicians and the heedless population of Jerusalem. No help would come from that quarter!

The terrible fate in store for the two prophets, Ahab and Zedekiah (20–23), agrees with Daniel 3 about Nebuchadrezzar's way of discouraging threats to his authority. What is said about their way of life adds one more potential mark of a false prophet to the various tests mentioned elsewhere in the Old Testament. These included: incitement to serve other gods (even when it was supported by signs and wonders and true predictions, Dt. 13:1–5); predictions that failed (Dt. 18:20–22, *cf.* Je. 28:9); indulgent preaching (Je. 23:17, 32); and here, immoral living (29:23).[47]

Threats from a prophet and a priest   29:24–32

The prophet Shemaiah, with his open letter to the populace, another to the priests, and a third to Zephaniah, the priest responsible for temple discipline, could hardly be accused of taking half-measures! But all this activity and blustering confessed his inability to meet his opponent's case on its merits. He should have known, too, that

---

[45] See the previous footnote.

[46] *Cf.* Jn. 17:3; 1 Cor. 2:9–10; Eph. 3:19; Phil. 3:8–16.

[47] In addition to adultery, the 'folly' here is that of the *nābāl*, the arrogant person portrayed in, *e.g.*, Ps. 14:1ff.; 1 Sa. 25:25.

the stocks (or pillory) had not silenced Jeremiah before,[48] nor would the addition of the iron collar.[49]

Of Zephaniah the priest, a successor to the brutal Pashhur-ben-Immer of chapter 20, we have only three glimpses apart from his arrest in 52:24, but they are enough to suggest a man picking his way between uncomfortable alternatives. Here he neither ignores Shemaiah's letter nor acts on it: it was safer simply to try its effect on Jeremiah. (Had his predecessor's fate[50] passed through his mind?) Yet after this inglorious encounter he is ready to be sent twice to Jeremiah by an unrepentant king[51] to solicit his prayers but not his preaching. Was he a career priest?

Jeremiah's reply (24, 30ff.) was addressed not only to Shemaiah himself (24) but to the exiles in general (31), since this was no private dispute but one on which their welfare turned. If we are tempted to view it as a merely instinctive counter-attack, we should note the differing prophecies addressed to different adversaries. Shemaiah, unlike the two prophets of verses 21ff. (who had made no threat against Jeremiah), is not promised a violent death: only that neither he nor his will live to see the restoration (32). Pashhur-ben-Immer, Jeremiah's persecutor, would witness the slaying of his companions, but would survive to die in Babylon and be buried there (20:4, 6). And so on. These were the varied decisions of God, as they professed to be; not thought-up equivalents of the degrees of personal injury received by the prophet.

The book of hope, part one   30:1 – 31:40

Even Isaiah rises to no greater heights of delighted eloquence than does Jeremiah in these chapters. The message is no longer to Judah alone but to *Israel and Judah* (30:3, 4); and there are moments when

---

[48] See 20:2ff., and comments on p. 79.
[49] *Cf.* JB, also K–B.
[50] *Cf.* 20:3, 6.
[51] See 21:1ff. and comments, p. 85; also 37:2–3, p. 122.

the northern tribes, under their name Ephraim, are specially consoled for their long chastening (31:18), and are seen returning eagerly to the Zion on which they had turned their back for centuries (31:6). Then, surpassing even the prospect of return and reunion, there emerges the promise of a new covenant (31:31ff.), in which the Old Testament itself would be transcended by the New.

Throughout this God-given dream (*cf.* 31:26) of things to come, the language and the landscape are those of Jeremiah's day, dominated by the theme of exile and restoration. Nevertheless a vaster ingathering than the modest one of 538 is foretold; and the covenant with Israel and Judah (31:31) would, in the event, embrace the world-wide 'sons of the living God', 'not from the Jews only but also from the Gentiles'.[52] Even the rebuilding of the city is envisaged in terms which outstrip the literal event, to draw the mind beyond the 'Jerusalem which now is' to 'Jerusalem which is above'.[53]

So, as elsewhere in prophecy, God had both an immediate and a distant prospect to unfold,[54] using language which spoke to the prophet's generation in the first place, but which pointed by its very exuberance to a greater fulfilment on a different plane: a secret 'hidden for ages and generations',[55] to be revealed only when its time arrived. *In the latter days*, says God to his people in this very prophecy, *you will understand this* (30:24c).

Good news to write down 30:1–3

All the words that I have spoken to you (2) refer evidently to these two chapters, 30 and 31, rather than to Jeremiah's whole output. (Chapter 36, covering that larger field, is introduced with a much fuller formula.)

Two things are made plain at once in this introduction: that the subject is the great homecoming,[56] and that it is meant for Israel as well as Judah, the north as well as the south. God had already made

---

[52] Rom. 9:24–26, *cf.* 1 Pet. 2:9–10.

[53] Gal. 4:25–26, AV, *cf.* Heb. 12:22ff.

[54] *Cf.*, *e.g.*, Ps. 2:7; Is. 7:14; Zc. 9:9; Mt. 24:15ff.

[55] *Cf.* Col. 1:25b–27; Jn. 12:16; 16:4.

[56] On the phrase 'restore the fortunes' (3), or 'turn again the captivity' (RV), see on 33:6ff., p. 114.

such a promise, early in Jeremiah's ministry (3:6–18): now he breaks into a series of poems to celebrate the theme.

But liberation is a costly business: its other face is judgment (4–11, 23–24), and the people to be liberated need saving from themselves as much as from their enemies (12–17). Such are the sombre realities that prepare for the radiance of chapter 31.

'A time of distress' 30:4–11

The fall of Babylon and the breaking of its *yoke*[57] were indeed to happen, but with far less upheaval than is depicted here. As for the promise of *David their king* (9), it would have to wait for the coming – indeed the coming in glory – of David's Lord. So at once we have a prophecy that looks far beyond the middle distance to the last days (see above, p. 90), both in its violent picture of *a day so great there is none like it* (7), and in its messianic vision of unbroken peace (8–10) to follow.

Meanwhile we see the balance of mercy and controlled severity in verse 11, a clause of which has already been heard in earlier prophecies: *but of you I will not make a full end.* Here, in the context of messianic prophecy, this promise comes as no surprise; but when it appeared at 4:27 and 5:10, 18 it came in passages that made reprieve almost unthinkable – so much so, that to some minds the clause had no right to be there.

Yet such is grace: never something that is due or obvious. If it ceases to surprise (this may remind us), it ceases to be known for what it is.

'Your guilt is great' 30:12–17

This paragraph, linked to the previous one by the word *For*,[58] enlarges on the theme of grace by dwelling on the hopeless and undeserving case that God was refusing to abandon. If the metaphor of desperate sickness evokes self-pity rather than self-blame, God will have none of it (15):

---

[57] See 27:2ff., 12ff.; 28:14.
[58] A connection omitted, regrettably, in NIV.

> *Why do you cry out over your hurt?...*
> *Because your guilt is great,*
>   *because your sins are flagrant,*
> *I have done these things to you.*

But the emphasis in verses 12 and 15 on what is incurable[59] and indefensible is preparing us for the paradox of verses 16–17, where God turns the tables on the enemy and retrieves the irretrievable, doing all this for his own honour – for he will not have it said of his people and his city that *no one cares* (17) for them!

This way of putting it is found most fully in Ezekiel 36:22ff., insisting that 'It is not for your sake ... that I am about to act, but for the sake of my holy name, which you have profaned among the nations ...' If that is unflattering to the sinner, it is all the more reassuring – for it overrides the question of human merit, which tends to creep back to undermine our thoughts of grace.

'Behold, I will restore...' 30:18–22

But it is much more than restoration! The idyllic picture of verses 8ff. is now filled out with detail, not only in terms of regaining all that had been lost (18–20) but of something new: a ruler *one of themselves*, who will be what no king had ever been allowed to be: their mediator and priest (21). It is one of the boldest but least-known messianic prophecies (for this ruler is clearly the 'David' of v.9):

> *Their prince shall be one of themselves,*
>   *their ruler shall come forth from their midst;*
> *I will make him draw near, and he shall approach me,*
>   *for who would dare*[60] *of himself to approach me?*

Once again God is lifting their eyes beyond the return from Babylon and the 'day of small things' (Zc. 4:10), to the promised priest-king whom David had foreseen, and whose benefits we now enjoy.[61]

Those benefits may be summed up in the quiet couplet of verse 22, which, with the radical simplicity of a marriage vow, has always expressed the heart of God's covenant, from Genesis to Revelation:

---

[59] This word in vv. 12 and 15 is the same as in 17:9 ('desperately corrupt').

[60] *Cf.* 2 Ch. 26:16–21.

[61] Ps. 110:4; Heb. 5:7–10; 7:11–28.

> *You shall be my people,*
> *and I will be your God.*[62]

Even the new heavens and new earth will be only the outskirts of what he has prepared. Here is the living centre.

Behold the storm of the Lord! 30:23–24

A chapter of alternating distress and delight closes aptly on the note that evil will not simply disappear: it must be punished and destroyed. In the short term, the Exile would be at least a token-punishment and partial purging of God's people, but ultimately punishment and purging must do their whole work everywhere, *until he has executed and accomplished the intents of his mind* (24).

In the latter days you will understand this (24c) – and the book of Revelation has now spelt it out, together with a glimpse of the new creation which will follow when, in Revelation's own words, 'It is done' (Rev. 21:5). Our next chapter expresses the sequel to the storm in terms that celebrate the promise of return from exile, but envisage a far greater gathering of the clans and return to the Lord than anything that happened at the liberation from Babylon.

A greater exodus 31:1–9

As in many passages of Isaiah,[63] the return from Babylon is pictured in terms that recall (and outdo) the exodus from Egypt. In our verse 2 *the wilderness* is such a word (*cf.* 2:2, where it referred directly to that time), but since 51:50 identifies *the people who survived the sword* as the exiles in Babylon, these latter-day pilgrims are promised, by implication, a journey no less divinely shepherded and completed than that of their fathers.

The fountain-head of the whole passage and of the whole chapter is the great saying of verse 3, *I have loved you with an everlasting love …* – for it is this, not any merit in the beloved, that has begun and will carry forward the relationship, through thick and thin, to its perfection. The opening line has already reminded us of this quality

---

[62] *Cf.* Gn. 17:7; Ex. 6:7; Lv. 26:12; Je. 31:33; Ho. 2:19, 23b; Rev. 21:3, 7.
[63] *E.g.* Is. 35; 41:17–20; 43:14–21; 48:20–21; 49:8–13.

by its words *from afar*, which speak not of divine aloofness but of human plight, as in 30:10,

> I will save you from afar,
> and your offspring from the land of their captivity.[64]

We can be reminded, too, of the spiritual dimension of this homelessness, perhaps to recall from another context the words, 'But when he was yet a great way off ...'[65]

The third line of this verse (3) is usually understood now as in RSV: *therefore I have continued*[66] *my faithfulness to you*. But the links with Hosea in this chapter, and the form of the sentence (see footnote) are quite strong arguments for the AV rendering, now supported by NIV: 'therefore with lovingkindness have I drawn thee', as in Hosea 11:4, AV, 'I drew them with cords of a man, with bands of love'. To such words the Song of Songs 1:4 (AV) suggests a suitably ardent response: 'Draw me, we will run after thee ...'

'Like a watered garden'   31:10–14

In terms of life's simple and occasional delights, such as reunion and security (10), a great deliverance (11), the abundance of nature (12), merrymaking (13) and feasting (14), God gives us a foretaste of final bliss: of joys that will no longer be fleeting or shadowed by fear. As ever, he uses the known to picture the unknown; but how satisfying the pictures are! 'It does not yet appear what we shall be',[67] but the flower that is in the bud here will be no disappointment when it opens.

No more tears   31:15–26

If we forget for the moment the famous quotation in Matthew 2:17–18,[68] the picture of Rachel weeping for her children speaks eloquently of the tragedy of the 'lost tribes' of Israel – for while

---

[64] *Cf.* also 51:50, 'Remember the Lord from afar, and let Jerusalem come into your mind'.

[65] Lk. 15:20, AV, *cf.* (addressed to Gentiles) Eph. 2:12–13.

[66] This verb, basically 'to pull', can mean 'prolong', as in Ps. 36:10 (11, Heb.). But the direct object is *prima facie* 'you' whom God has 'pulled' (*i.e.*, 'drawn', 'attracted'); and the word 'faithfulness' (*ḥeseḏ*, steadfast love, lovingkindness) can be used adverbially: 'with faithfulness' *etc.*

[67] 1 Jn. 3:2.

[68] On this, see the Additional Notes, p. 108f.

Benjamin had stayed with Judah when the kingdom split up, Rachel's other descendants, the 'Joseph tribes' of Ephraim and Manasseh, had been the backbone of the breakaway kingdom. That kingdom ('Israel' or 'Ephraim') had vanished into exile more than a century before.

But Rachel can dry her tears, for the excellent reason that (in the prophet's vision) *Ephraim* has at last begun to mourn not for his fate but for his sins (18–19). It is a kind of sequel to the book of Hosea, whose picture of Ephraim as a stubborn heifer,[69] or a rebellious son who breaks his father's heart,[70] comes powerfully to mind in our verses 18–20, not least for its variations on the Hebrew for 'to turn'.[71] Like Hosea, Jeremiah uses this word both for the sinner's turning away (19) and for his turning back in repentance and conversion (18c) – here seen as something only God can really bring about: '*bring* me back ...' Then, and only then, will the literal return *to these your cities* (21) be worth the journey.

So far, this chapter has been a song for Ephraim, and with good reason, since these northern Israelites had seemed to have disappeared for good. But verses 23–25 make sure that Judah knows itself equally in need of and in prospect of this restoring and reunion – although the fact of Zion as Israel's rallying point (6, 12) had left no reasonable doubt of it. To the whole people, and to 'every' member of it, the final couplet offers the Lord's personal welcome home (25):

> For I will satisfy the weary soul,
> and every languishing soul I will replenish.

Small wonder that to awake on such a note (26) and to look around at the scene of his own day was to make the contrast poignant. But notice that Jeremiah remarks not that such a contrast spoils everything, but that it enhances the delights he has glimpsed in vision. As with thoughts of heaven, the former reaction is crippling; the latter uplifting.

ADDITIONAL NOTES ON 31:15 and 31:22

31:15 How did the weeping for the massacre of the innocents

[69] Ho. 4:16.
[70] Ho. 7:15; 11:1–2, 8–9.
[71] See also on 15:19, p. 69.

(Mt. 2:17–18) 'fulfil' this oracle? It is a question for a commentary on Matthew; but as a tentative reply we may note that in Matthew 2 we are pointed to Jesus as the one upon whom the Old Testament's lines converge: the Christ (Mt. 2:1–6); the true Son, with the true Exodus to accomplish (Mt. 2:15); the greater than Moses (Mt. 2:20 echoing Ex. 4:19); the *nēṣer* ('branch', Is. 11:1) suggested by the name Nazarene (Mt. 2:23); and at Matthew 2:17–18, the one whose disturbing presence brought yet another draught of suffering to a tragic people. The mothers of Bethlehem, like Rachel the mother of the Joseph tribes, could only weep; yet our passage tells us that Rachel's tears were not in vain and not for ever (31:16–17). Did the gospel's allusion to it hint at the same long view? 'There is hope for your future, says the Lord, and your children shall come back ...' (17) – these to a better country than they had lost.

31:22 'For the Lord has created a new thing on the earth: a woman protects a man.' 'Protects' is lit. 'encompasses', and it has an affectionate tone in the comparable contexts: Deuteronomy 32:10; Psalm 32:7, 10. The Hebrew word for it, *t^esôḇēḇ*, also somewhat resembles the word *šôḇēḇā* ('unfaithful', NIV; 'wayward', NEB) earlier in the verse, perhaps in pointed contrast to it. So, among the many suggestions offered for this saying, I am drawn to reading it as a foretaste of the new covenant of verses 31ff., with the new intimacy between the Lord and his bride – hitherto a one-sided cherishing of his unresponsive partner, but henceforth an affection that is fully mutual.

Perhaps, too, there is a hint of the unexpected 'weakness of God':[72] the scandalous defencelessness that the mighty one[73] would accept in the incarnation, childhood, ministry and death of Christ, reversing the apparent roles of Yahweh and his bride as protector and protected, sustainer and sustained.

It may well be, however, that all this is to overpress the details of what should be seen as a proverbial saying for anything novel and incredible: simply an underlining of the announcement that God was planning 'a new thing'; in particular, the new covenant of verses 31ff.

---

[72] *Cf.* 1 Cor. 1:23–25; 2 Cor. 13:4.
[73] The word for 'a man' here emphasizes his strength; *cf.* 'mighty', from the same root, in Is. 9:6 (9:5, Heb.).

A fresh start 31:27–30

To appreciate the good news of this, we need to remember the eerie picture of a deserted landscape in 4:23–28, and God's opening call to Jeremiah to *pluck up and to break down, to destroy and to overthrow* (just as in v. 28 here) before he might 'build and plant' (1:10). Here at last the site is cleared, the land is waiting; here too is freedom from the past. Verses 29–30 are often cited as newly introducing the truth of individual responsibility, as though it had been scarcely known before. But the context is of farewell to defeatism and to excuses: the past is dealt with, the future beckons. As ever, each person counts and will be held accountable; but there is better news of this than hitherto, to be unfolded in the great announcement that now follows.

A new covenant 31:31–34

The old covenant had taken a new lease of life in Jeremiah's early days, when the lost 'book of the covenant'[74] was found and read and reaffirmed, to become the blueprint of Josiah's continuing reformation. Yet everything that we have read in Jeremiah confirms that 'the law made nothing perfect',[75] for the response was skin-deep, and died with the death of Josiah.

This, then, was God's moment to speak of a covenant that would be heart-deep and everlasting.[76] As with all God's covenants, it would come of his initiative, not ours (notice *I will make*[77] ... *I will put* ... *I will write* ..., *etc.*), and the relationship it would establish is summed up in the words *I will be their God, and they shall be my people* (33c; *cf.* the comments and references at 30:22, p. 105).

But since a marriage (note the words, *though I was their husband*, 32) can be either an uneasy yoke or else a love-match, God makes sure of the latter with his three gifts of grace: a love of his will, a one-to-one relationship with every believer, and a full forgiveness of the past. What would only come to light when Jesus inaugurated this new covenant (Mt. 26:28), was the fact that each of these divine gifts was a costly *self*-giving. Forgiveness would be through his own

---

[74] 2 Ch. 34:30.
[75] Heb. 7:19.
[76] See not only 31:33–34, but 32:40.
[77] Lit., 'I will cut...' On this expression, see the comments on 34:18–19, p. 117.

blood, and it would be not only the law but its Author who would indwell the believer (Jn. 14:17, 23).

On neither side could this be an arm's-length transaction. But what capricious hospitality the divine guest would be accepting!

> Come, not to find, but make, this troubled heart
> A dwelling worthy of Thee as Thou art;
> To chase the gloom, the terror and the sin,
> Come, all Thyself, yea come, Lord Jesus, in!
>
> H. C. G. Moule

God of the farthest and nearest   31:35–40

From the cosmic to the commonplace is a typical Old Testament plunge – or is it a soaring to the true pinnacle? In this passage the order, power and scale of the Creator's world are but tokens of his fidelity in the *personal* realm (36–37) – and in verses 38–40 the promise is therefore 'earthed' not merely in this planet but in the familiar details of Israel's capital, naming rubbish dumps and all.

As for these details, the prophecy is again using the known and the near to project an image of the ultimate. The city would indeed be rebuilt, and we read in Nehemiah 3:1 of the tower of Hananel as situated near the starting-point of that operation, as Nehemiah's account works its way westward from the north-east corner, turning south at presumably the Corner Gate,[78] eventually to come northwards up the east side, via the Horse Gate (Ne. 3:28) to complete the circuit.

But the vision outruns that exercise, in scale and in significance. *The measuring line shall go out farther* (39), not turning at the Corner Gate; and the places that were once unclean *shall be sacred to the Lord* (40). Added to these things, the promise that the city would never again be overthrown (40c) is a further sign that we must look beyond 'the present Jerusalem' to 'the Jerusalem above' (Gal. 4:25–26): the great company of saints and angels which is already our home city, as seen in, *e.g.*, Hebrews 12:22–24; Revelation 21:1 – 22:5.

The Hebrews passage adds the exhortation: 'Therefore let us be grateful for receiving a kingdom which cannot be shaken, and thus

---

[78] Mentioned here (38) and at 2 Ki. 14:13; Zc. 14:10.

let us offer to God acceptable worship, with reverence and awe ...'
(Heb. 12:28).

The book of hope, part two   32:1 – 33:26

We are now projected into the year 588/7, only months before the
fall of a starving and plague-ridden Jerusalem (32:24), and with
Jeremiah now in prison (32:2; 33:1). What has led up to this will be
told in subsequent chapters; but these two are placed here no doubt
to reinforce the buoyant prophecies of chapters 30 – 31, by showing
in sober prose how unpromising, humanly speaking, were the
conditions in which such words from God were spoken, and with
what conviction they were stood by.

Jeremiah buys an inheritance   32:1–15

Everything here reveals the man of faith, not of unconsidered
impulse. The outspokenness which had put Jeremiah in custody
(3–5) is now matched by his humble openness to what God might
have in mind to say to him there. So instead of meeting his cousin's
untimely proposition (8) with hurt and anger (was there ever a more
insensitive prison-visitor?), his reaction was *Then I knew that this was
the word of the Lord* (8c). Since the early, doubt-ridden days[79] he has
learnt, and still teaches the rest of us, to recognize the hidden hand
of God in what befalls him, from whatever human quarter it may
arise.

In fact, the very meanness of his cousin's pressure on him as
next-of-kin[80] gave Jeremiah his opportunity to have his visions of
the future taken seriously. To buy land overrun by the world's
conqueror, and then to take elaborate care of the title-deeds (9–15)[81]
was a striking affirmation, as solid as the silver that paid for it, that
God would bring his people back to their inheritance (15).

---

[79] *E.g.*, 15:18; 20:7.

[80] For the rights and duties of the nearest kinsman, see Lv. 25:25ff.

[81] The 2,000-year preservation of the Dead Sea Scrolls makes its own comment on v.14b.

A *confession of perplexity*   32:16–25

After the bold gesture, a daring plea – for Jeremiah is quick to explore the possibility that God might be opening a door of last-minute mercy for Jerusalem. The beginning (17) and the end (25) of his prayer contain the substance of it, in the opening cry, *Nothing is too hard for thee* (17c),[82] and in the probing of verse 25 into the paradox of God's simultaneous yes and no: the 'yes' implied in the purchase just completed, and the 'no' implied in the rapidly collapsing city.

It is a fine example of the way to pray in a desperate situation: concentrating first on the creative power (17) and perfect fidelity and justice (18–19) of God; remembering next his great redemptive acts (20–23a; to which the Christian can now add the greatest of them all) – and then with this background, laying before God the guilt of the past (23b), the hard facts of the present (24) and the riddle of the future (25).

The Lord's *two-stage reply*   32:26–44

Although God takes up Jeremiah's 'Nothing is too hard for thee' (27, *cf.* 17), with its reminder that the very existence of his people rested on a miracle,[83] he immediately kills the idea of miracles as an escape from moral facts. Indeed, his *Therefore* ... (28) announces that the omnipotence which Jeremiah's prayer invoked will empower the attackers, not the defenders (it is put more strongly still at 37:10!). The guilt that called for this judgment could hardly have been more broadly based (notice the wide cross-section of society in v.32), or more persistent (30–31, 33) or more flagrant – culminating in the child-sacrifice for which even the ancient Canaanites had been expelled from Canaan.[84]

But having said this, God paints a glowing picture of the great reversal (vv. 37ff.), repeating and even amplifying the promises of chapter 31. Not only will the covenant be new, as promised there, but *everlasting* (40); and meanwhile – keeping this bit to the end for

---

[82] An echo of God's historic words to Abraham in Gn. 18:14.

[83] Gn. 18:14.

[84] Dt. 12:29–31; 18:10–12. See also the comment on Je. 19:5, p. 79.

Jeremiah's benefit — there will be fields bought here, there and everywhere, in places probable and improbable; and deeds galore, all sealed and witnessed as carefully as Jeremiah's own: each one a vindication of his gallant act of faith and of the Lord's delight *in doing [his people] good, ... with all [his] heart and all [his] soul* (41).

Seventeen shekels of silver (9) were surely never better spent.

'The voice of mirth and the voice of gladness'   33:1–13

It was typical of the Lord, whose angels or whose own presence would strengthen other hard-pressed servants at their darkest moments,[85] that he should now bring a second message to the imprisoned Jeremiah. It is also rather striking that his opening word is not a bare announcement but an invitation: *Call to me and I will answer you,*[86] *and will tell you great and hidden things which you have not known* (3). In other words, although God can make himself heard, and has already done so in saying this, nevertheless to reveal all that he wants to say, he desires a hearer who is already reaching out to him. This is why prayer is never superfluous to the study of Scripture or the quest for guidance. God is then speaking to an upturned face, not a preoccupied back.

The promises that follow (6ff.) fill out the picture of restored fortunes,[87] as seen in chapters 30 – 32, adding in verse 9 the prospect of a world impressed by these events, and in verses 10–11 a happy variation at last on Jeremiah's frequent theme of streets that should hum with cheerful sounds.[88]

Never to lack a rightful king and rightful priests   33:14–26

However prosperous, a people kingless and without a priesthood would consider itself no better than a rabble: so here is the climax of

---

[85] *Cf.* Mt. 4:11; Lk. 22:43; Acts 23:11; 27:23.

[86] The 'you' is singular throughout this verse.

[87] The expression, 'restore the fortunes' (*šûḇ š'ḇûṯ*) is almost a refrain in these chapters (29:14; 30:3, 18; 31:23; 32:44; 33:7, 11, 26). The older translations derive the second Heb. word from the root 'to take captive', hence 'turn the captivity'. But since some contexts are not of captivity (*e.g.* Jb. 42:10), it may be that both its Heb. words are from the root 'to turn' (on which, see on 31:18–21): *i.e.*, 'reverse the reversal', in other words 'restore the fortunes'. To a people threatened with captivity, however, there would be little difference between the two possible senses, as J. Bright points out (Bright, p. 278).

[88] See comment and references at 16:9.

the promise. The messianic prophecy of 23:5 is repeated; but now the promise of the Lord's saving righteousness[89] is extended to cover not only the king but the very city that had once been called 'Zion, for whom no one cares'.[90]

As for the pledge that David would *never lack a man to sit on the throne of ... Israel* (17, 21a), we can see how profoundly the fulfilment in the person of Christ transcends the expectation (Rev. 11:15; 22:16). The same is true of the promise to the Levitical priests, since all their atoning work was done to perfection and for eternity by him, and their role in offering 'the sacrifice of praise' has been perpetuated and extended in the royal priesthood of believers. That company, from the earliest days of the church, has always included literal descendants of the priestly tribe of Levi,[91] but the Old Testament itself foresaw the opening of their closed circle to the converted from all nations;[92] and the book of Revelation can describe the completed church both symbolically in terms of the perfected twelve tribes of Israel (Rev. 7:3–8; 14:1–5), and literally as 'a great multitude ... from every nation' (Rev. 7:9ff.).

In our passage, however, the promise contains no hint of the hidden elements in its fulfilment, but (as A. W. Streane puts it) is 'clothed in a Jewish dress, the only form in which it could present any meaning to those to whom it was delivered'. The same author adds: 'It is no doubt to such passages as this that St. Peter refers (1 Pet. i. 10, 11), when he speaks of the prophets as "enquiring and searching diligently ... what or what manner of time the Spirit of Christ which was in them did signify, when it testified beforehand the sufferings of Christ, *and the glory that should follow*".'[93]

---

[89] See comment and footnote to 23:5.

[90] 30:17b, but *cf.* 33:9a.

[91] *Cf.* Acts 4:36; 6:7.

[92] Is. 66:21. For the understanding of 'some of them' as referring to the converted among the Gentiles, see, *e.g.*, Delitzsch, *Isaiah, ad loc.*; C. Westermann, *Isaiah 40 – 66* (SCM, 1969), *ad loc.*

[93] Streane, p. 229 (his italics).

Promise-breakers and promise-keepers 34:1 – 35:19

The promise-breakers 34:1–22

The time is a little earlier than that of chapters 32 – 33, since Jeremiah is not yet in prison (*Go and speak...*, 2). In verses 1–7 the siege has begun in earnest, with only two cities besides Jerusalem still holding out; but verses 8–22 tell of what happened when a threat from Egypt against the invaders provided a temporary respite (21b, *cf.* 37:5). This was in early or mid-588, about a year before the fall of the city.

Small comfort for the king 34:1–7

This vacillating king, whose treachery to his overlord[94] and fear of his own subjects[95] made him a broken reed to anyone who had to deal with him, is given enough warning to save him from prolonging his city's agony, and at least a crumb of consolation about his own future (4–5).[96] In the event, he lacked the courage to act on the implied advice to surrender, either now or when it was repeated at 38:17 with a generous promise added to it. As for his own fate, the prophecy of verse 3 spared him the foreknowledge of what Nebuchadrezzar would do to him when they met (39:6–7; 52:10–11), although Ezekiel in Babylonia foretold the substance of it to his people (Ezk. 12:13). Remembering the readiness of God to take back a threat (18:8, 11), and the clemency of Nebuchadrezzar to Jeremiah for his advocacy of surrender (39:11–12), we may wonder whether even now Zedekiah might have found mercy had he repented.

---

[94] 2 Ki. 24:17–20; Ezk. 17:11–21.
[95] Je. 38:5, 19.
[96] *Cf.*, in contrast, the ignominious end of Jehoiakim, 22:18–19.

The perfidious slave-owners   34:8–22

A *proclamation of liberty* for slaves (8), ratified before God (15), shines at first sight like a good deed in a naughty world – until perhaps King Zedekiah's name to it arouses our misgivings. It was all very scriptural (14, *cf*. Dt. 15:12), but this unaccustomed zeal coincided with the pinch of famine and the inconvenience of having many mouths to feed. No doubt people told themselves that slaves could forage for themselves better on their own – it is the kind of argument which most of us know how to use.

If this was disingenuous, what followed was wicked. The siege was raised, the enemy withdrew to fight off the Egyptians (21b; 37:5) – and now there was no longer a food problem but a servant problem. So the release of slaves was cancelled, and these unfortunates were back where they had started.

What the cynics forgot was that the last word is with God. Here it was expressed first with the irony of verse 17, saying in effect, 'It's for me now to do some liberating, as you refused to. *You* can go out – to the predators.' But the main charge was concerning the covenant, *which* (says God) *they made before me* (18). Here, in verses 18–19,[97] we are given our clearest glimpse of the solemn rite that evidently gave rise to the expression, to 'cut'[98] a covenant, and of the meaning it conveyed. The carcase of the covenant-sacrifice was cut in two, and the two parts placed opposite one another so that the parties to the covenant could pass between them. Whatever else this was taken to symbolize, verse 18 indicates that it invoked against a covenant-breaker a like fate to that of the sacrificial victim.

Some covenants were agreements between equals, but in this example only the owners *passed between the parts* (19). In the covenant with Abram, only the fire of the Lord did so (Gn. 15:17–18), for the divine covenants are gifts to be accepted, not deals to be negotiated. They are comparable to a will and its bequests.[99] God's indignation at this example of a broken covenant leaves us in no doubt of the sacredness of his own commitment:

---

[97] *Cf*. Gn. 15:9–10, 17–18.

[98] This is the word translated 'made' in vv. 8, 13, 15, 18. In the Heb. of v. 18 both the covenant and the calf are 'cut'.

[99] Hebrews 9:15–18 draws on the double meaning of the Gk. *diathēkē*, 'covenant' or 'will', which is the word used in the LXX (rather than *synthēkē*, 'contract') to translate the Heb. word for covenant.

Though years on years roll on,
His covenant shall endure;
Though clouds and darkness hide his path,
The promised grace is sure.

(J. Wesley, after P. Gerhardt)

The promise-keepers: the Rechabites   35:1–19

Although this chapter returns us to the reign of Jehoiakim (609–598), its placing here makes the sharpest of comments on the promise-breakers of chapter 34.

The Rechabites, these spartan characters, saw themselves as living witnesses to the pilgrim origins of Israel, shunning the settled life of farms and vineyards for the simplicities of tents and flocks. Their ancestor, Jonadab, had not only set them this pattern: he was the zealot who had joined with Jehu in setting up that king's notorious massacre of Baal-worshippers.[100] All this had happened some two-and-a-half centuries ago, but the years had done nothing to weaken the family's tradition.

In this test of their conservatism everything was arranged to maximize the pressure on them. The gathering of the whole clan (3), the exalted meeting-place (4), and the hospitable provision (5) which it would seem churlish to refuse, all contributed to the persuasiveness of so special an occasion. Added to this was doubtless the family's consciousness of having already accepted one compromise by moving into the safety of Jerusalem (11). Not the least of these pressures, perhaps, was the spiritual prestige of Jeremiah, their host – for godly people tend to take their cue from the example of a respected leader when it comes to questions of revising old patterns of behaviour. First Jonadab, now Jeremiah?

It may have been a surprise to Jeremiah when *the word of the Lord came* to him (12) about the Rechabites' refusal. For all he knew, his task had been indeed to wean them away from the eccentric lifestyle, humanly imposed on them, which was isolating them from the present and from their fellows. Their rebuff for his approach surely invited (he might suppose) a corresponding rebuke from heaven.

So the drama had possibly a twist in the tail, certainly a moral nobody could miss. Verse 16 was now projected with uncomfortable

---

[100] 2 Ki. 10:15–27.

force: *The sons of Jonadab ... have kept the command which their father gave them, but this people has not obeyed me.* And its sequel, in the *Therefore ...* of verse 17, was all the darker for the bright promise (18–19) to those obstinate puritans who, as everyone knew, needed dragging into the sixth century!

Incidentally, as a secondary thrust of this episode, we are reminded that God, who loves unity and truth, is no lover of uniformity. By his own order of Nazirites[101] he called some people, but not others, to an austerity not unlike that of the Rechabites, to make a particular point; and the fact that Jesus and John the Baptist glorified God by different lifestyles[102] should open our minds to the reality and value of specialized callings – such as even the once-flourishing temperance movement which adopted the name of Rechabites in nineteenth-century England.

A day that sold the future   36:1–32

A national appeal   36:1–3

The dramatic adventures of the scroll should not distract us from what was at stake on this fateful day, when king and people set their course towards the shipwreck of their kingdom, nearly twenty years distant. God's statement of intent in verse 3 endorses what he had revealed at the potter's house about the provisional nature of all prophecy,[103] and it still applies to us. Why else should he pour out threats rather than immediate actions, unless it is to bring us to our senses and to his feet? Why make promises, unless it is to rouse us to the partnership of trust? The issues, then as now, were no less than life and death for a prejudiced and preoccupied generation.

---

[101] Nu. 6:1–21.
[102] Lk. 7:31–35. *Cf.* the variations between Gentile and Jewish churches defended in 1 Cor. 9:19–23, and between individual believers in Rom. 14:6.
[103] Je. 18:5–12.

A faithful scribe   36:4–8

Baruch ('Blessed'), to whom we probably owe the editing and the narrative framework of the completed book, knew that he risked his career, if not his life, by what he was to write down and read out – for the little chapter 45 belongs to this moment. There we overhear his piteous protest and the Lord's quiet rebuke and reassurance. Baruch accepted it, to our lasting benefit.

The process described in verse 4 (*cf.* vv. 17–18) is no more than we should expect, but it does make crystal-clear the claim that this document contained no mere selection, but *all*; no paraphrase relying on the scribe's impressions or his memory (*cf.* v.18, 'He dictated ... while I wrote them'); and no mere outpouring of the prophet's views, but *the words of the Lord which he had spoken to him*. It was this that gave Jeremiah reason to hope that the reading, bypassing the authorities, might bring about a massed repentance – for only the word of God can cut as deep as this.

The first two readings   36:9–19

We hear of no popular reaction to the public reading: only the concern of one man, Micaiah (11–13), the son of the owner of the room used for the occasion. If there were others touched, they were few, for there was no general repentance such as verse 7 had looked for, despite the outward solemnity of the fast-day (9) on which the reading took place. Perhaps the external act was felt to be piety enough – for we have already seen that sacraments meant more to this generation than words from God (6:19–20).

The second reading, to the *princes*,[104] or high officials, found a responsive audience (see the vivid v.16a), for it was laymen such as these, and perhaps the same men, who had saved Jeremiah from death for his 'Shiloh' sermon not long before (26:1, 16). Three of them, Elnathan, Delaiah and Gemariah, would speak up, later that day, at a dangerous moment; and Gemariah had already declared himself by lending his room for the public reading. What is also impressive about these men is their careful enquiry into the nature of this document: whether each word of it was authentic or not (17).

---

[104] This word, *śārîm*, was not a term for members of the royal family, who were simply termed 'the king's sons', as in v.26a.

As soon as they were satisfied of this, they knew what they must do, and did it.

Scripture to the flames 36:20–26

So to the third reading. It is an extraordinary scene. The king's slow, methodical destruction of the scroll, keeping pace with the steady progress of the reading, made his rejection a far more emphatic gesture than a swift reaction in hot blood. But his further step in ordering the arrest of Baruch and Jeremiah (26) revealed the fury and perhaps the fear beneath the show of cool defiance. Whatever his view of the prophecies,[105] he was taking no risks with the prophet and his kind. Such men might influence the ignorant. Even at court, the protests of the three princes (25) were proof enough that the yes-men of verse 24 were not the only types that he must reckon with.

The scroll reissued 36:27–32

This first recorded attempt to obliterate the word of God is something of a foretaste of the attacks on it in days to come: by sceptics, by persecutors, and, with whatever good intent, by the rash use of the scholar's knife. On this occasion, as on others to come, God saw to its preservation and completion (32); and it is interesting to reflect that behind the king's bravado (and behind that of some later assailants) there may have lurked an unacknowledged fear. Was it *only* to express contempt that he reduced the scroll to ashes? Or was it, rather, the kind of precaution that a superstitious man cannot quite bring himself to renounce, whatever his disclaimers? Did he reckon that these words were dangerous as long as they remained in writing?

What he could not reach with knife and fire was, of course, their Author: yet all the time (as we saw from v.3) it was the Author who was reaching out to him and to his people. The reading had said as much, especially in 18:1–11; but the king was not listening: his mind was made up.

'How often would I ..., and you would not!'[106]

---

[105] Yet see below.
[106] Mt. 23:37.

The last days of Jerusalem   37:1 – 39:18

After the various previews that we have had of episodes in Jerusalem's death-throes – glimpses given to illuminate the message rather than the sequence of events[107] – the next three chapters take us forward from the temporary lifting of the siege in, it seems, the summer of 588, to the fall of the city in July 587; telling chiefly of Jeremiah's successive imprisonments and of King Zedekiah's painfully irresolute dealings with him.

False hopes and false arrest   37:1–21

A deputation to Jeremiah   37:1–10

This was the second of two very similar approaches to the prophet within a short time.[108] In the first, the king had asked him to pray for a miraculous raising of the siege, only to receive God's terrifying answer: 'I myself will fight against you' (21:5). Now, however, the siege *has* been raised, thanks to a military threat from Egypt (5), and the king is emboldened to try again for God's favour (3). But Jeremiah has already been told to stop praying against defeat;[109] and in any case we know from chapter 34 that king and people have just been celebrating their good fortune by rearresting their slaves, to God's intense displeasure. The incongruity of the king's pious *Pray for us...* at such a moment – not for pardon, only for peace – was doubtless lost on him, as such incongruities often are on the rest of us. Isaiah 1:10–20 has some comments on this kind of phenomenon.

---

[107] Ch. 21 belongs to the first stage of the siege, early 588 BC, before the brief lifting of the siege. Chs. 27 – 28, long before this, are from Zedekiah's fourth year, c.594, with ch. 29 also early in his reign. Ch. 32 told of Jeremiah's imprisonment in the court of the guard (cf. 37:21; 38:13), begun during the respite from siege, probably in the summer of 588. Ch. 34 gives another angle on that respite.

[108] For comments on the earlier deputation, see on ch. 21, p. 85. The present pair of delegates is as unpromising as the first, consisting of Zephaniah as before (21:1; 29:25–29), and J(eh)ucal, who would help to consign Jeremiah to the deepest dungeon (38:1, 6).

[109] E.g., 7:16; 14:11.

Jeremiah is flogged and jailed   37:11–15

We know no details of the property which Jeremiah was on his way to claim (12), for this was distinct from the portion he was later asked to buy from a relative, as recounted in 32:6ff. (see p. 112). By then, he was in prison (32:2); here, he is about to be arrested.

There was every excuse for the sentry's suspicion that Jeremiah was a deserter, in view of his advice to others,[110] but less excuse for his and the princes' refusal to accept his denial. It was, of course, an odd thing to point others to safety while refusing it for oneself; but such was Jeremiah's calling from God, if they could believe in such an unseen constraint. So began his 'passion', if we may borrow such a term to remind us of this faint foreshadowing of his Master's suffering, of whom it would be said, 'He saved others; himself he cannot save.'[111]

The king sends for Jeremiah   37:16–21

While this first place of imprisonment was not as filthy as that of 38:6, it was a dungeon none the less, and such as to bring Jeremiah near to dying (20b). Did the king hope that the ordeal of *many days* would have broken his spirit by the time he sent for him? Certainly Jeremiah was dreading a return to this place of slow death (20), but his prophetic voice was unwavering. From his abrupt reply, *There is* (it was a monosyllable), in answer to the king's *Is there any word from the Lord?*, on to his bare announcement of the king's fate in four short Hebrew words (17b), he showed himself the same spokesman for God as ever. Only then did he turn to his own case – with another shrewd blow for true prophecy (19) – and end with his *humble plea* for better conditions. That plea, incidentally, was going to provide the king with useful camouflage (38:26), but at least he granted it and a little more besides (21). For whatever reasons in addition to compassion (and Zedekiah's motives will have been as mixed as most of ours), the king did not want the death of this man of God on his hands.

[110] *E.g.*, 21:8–10; 38:2.
[111] Mt. 27:42, AV.

Cowardice or courage?   38:1–28

Into the miry pit   38:1–6

Only if we hold the view that a soldier, a fortress or an army should never surrender, even when all is lost, can we join the princes in calling Jeremiah a traitor. All was indeed lost, as God announced (3), and Jerusalem's suicidal stand had not even a tactical value, now that the whole country was overrun and the Egyptian thrust had failed. Only obstinacy, at whatever cost in lives, could prolong the agony; and it was obstinacy not only against the enemy but against the Lord, in whose name (not his own) Jeremiah was calling for these surrenders (2). It was ironical, we might add, that the leaders who had played the traitor against Babylon, their overlord, were such sticklers for internal loyalty, and that they should profess concern for the peace and welfare (shalom, v.4b) of the citizens whom they insisted on sacrificing.

The king's capitulation to his princes (5) was perhaps the most abject surrender in biblical history (while we are on the subject of surrenders) until the moment when Pilate washed his hands before the multitude (Mt. 27:24). The consigning of Jeremiah to the mud pit was intended as a gradual and revolting death (see v.4a); but the king wanted no knowledge of it; and the princes, lowering their victim by ropes, took care to let death arrive by natural causes. Such evasions, and their milder counterparts common to us all, are no true escapes. Pilate only immortalized his cowardice. Zedekiah would find that it was he rather than the prophet whose feet were 'sunk in the mire', as Jeremiah pointed out (22).

The African rescuer   38:7–13

Of the friends who stood by Jeremiah,[112] none was braver or more determined than this palace official from Ethiopia or the Sudan.[113] The king, he knew, was easily swayed, but would be of little help against the wrath of the princes. No matter. His urgency shows in the heightened picture he paints: something like 'He's dead with

[112] See on 26:24, p. 97, and on ch. 45, p. 135.

[113] He is called lit. 'the Cushite' (*cf.* NIV), and Cush is the word regularly translated as Ethiopia in AV, *etc.*, following LXX. But it is more likely to refer to the region of Nubia and northern Sudan.

hunger there!' – nor did he pause to reflect that to say *there is no bread left in the city* would hardly strengthen his case for taking steps to avert the man's starvation.[114]

But love spoke louder than logic, and prevailed. Above all, it humanized the help it gave, as seen in the famous recourse to 'old cast clouts and old rotten rags' (11,AV). Even David the psalmist never pictured such a detail as he reflected on his rescue in Psalm 40:2! – yet he almost says it in Psalm 18:16, 35b (AV):

> He sent from above, he took me,
>> he drew me out of many waters...
> and thy gentleness hath made me great.

King and prophet: the last encounter 38:14–28

From the court of the guard, where he would remain now to the fall of the city,[115] Jeremiah is brought to the king in secret, this time at the temple. He knows all too well that Zedekiah is only hoping for a change of mind in God, instead of the change on his own part that he cannot face. He also knows what poor security a solemn oath (16) from this man amounts to (in inverse ratio, as often happens, to the strength of his language).[116]

Yet the inspired reply (17–23) offered mercy at this late hour, on the very terms that God had offered to individuals who surrendered,[117] now extended to the city itself and to the king – rebel though he was – and his family. It was an astounding invitation, all the more so for the previous withholding of all hope for Jerusalem,[118] apart from hope for its rebuilding (*e.g.*, 30:18; 31:38). To see what hung on the king's yes or no, we have only to read the next chapter for the horror awaiting him and his sons, or to read Lamentations 4 for the living skeletons and cannibals of the city's last days. With suffering on this scale in the balance, the king's reply in verse 19 is unbelievably trifling.[119] Yet God's answer

---

[114] Supplies did not quite run out until the final day (52:6). On the other hand, the army would commandeer everything it could. Without his allotted ration at the court of the guard (37:21), Jeremiah was destitute.

[115] 38:13, 28; 39:14.

[116] *Cf.* Mt. 5:37; Jas. 5:12.

[117] 21:8–10; 38:2–3.

[118] Among many oracles, see esp. 37:9–10.

[119] Yet Zedekiahs are, tragically, no rarity in relation to eternity: choosing between its infinitely bigger issues on grounds often remarkably like his.

125

to it still holds the door open with a characteristic pair of options: to dare to say yes, and be free; or to say a coward's no and be helpless – with no kind Ebed-melech to haul him up from his pit:

> *now that your feet are sunk in the mire,*
> *they turn away from you* (22).

Even the preview of what he is bringing on his family (23) fails to pull the king together. Like a child, he is only scared of having his secret talk found out. His parting words – virtually, 'Don't tell on me!' – show that God's latest and last call to turn back from the brink (20ff.) has not even registered with him.

So the conversation dies, with nothing more profound for Jeremiah to tell the princes than an unimportant extract from an old interview.[120] On that note of anticlimax the fate of a kingdom is left to take care of itself.

The city falls   39:1–18

Further details of the city's capture and of the aftermath are given in chapter 52, with special reference to the removal of the temple treasures. Here, after the fate of the king, the chief interest lies in what was in store for the prophet and for his rescuer, Ebed-melech.

Siege, fall and flight   39:1–7

So the siege lasted for eighteen months, from 10 January 588[121] to 9 July 587, interrupted briefly by the respite recorded in 37:5ff. The breaching of the walls (2) coincided with the final failure of the food supply, as we learn from 52:6 – which suggests that the defences were manned to the last gasp.

Zedekiah, who has not dared to let God save him and his city and his family (38:17–19), now deserts the people he has doomed. His flight, like his lifelong flight from reality, could have only one outcome. Nothing that his overbearing ministers or subjects might have done to him (38:5, 19) could compare with the revenge that

---

[120] *Cf.* vv. 26–27 with 37:20.

[121] The Hebrew year began in April, or more precisely March-April. The start of the siege was revealed to Ezekiel in Babylonia with tragic emphasis (Ezk. 24:1–2, 15–18) and was commemorated by fasting (along with the events of our v.2 and of 41:1–3 and 52:12) throughout the Exile – but not for ever, in God's intention: see Zc. 8:19.

Nebuchadrezzar would take; but this was the pattern of all his choices and their outcome, making him a supreme example of our Lord's paradox that safety is a fatal goal to live for.[122] If we would judge him, we may be judging ourselves, for his weakness might never have revealed itself had he not been thrust into a position that was far beyond him.

The Bible's verdict and sentence on him is stern but touched with mercy. He is utterly condemned for his perfidy ('Can a man escape who does such things? Can he break the covenant and yet escape?'[123]), yet he was spared the ignominy of dying unlamented like his bullying brother Jehoiakim (cf. 22:18–19). He was to die blinded and in exile, as Ezekiel 12:13 predicted; but in peace and with the mourning rites proper to a king – 'For I have spoken the word, says the Lord.'[124]

The kingdom dismantled   39:8–10

Chapter 52 expands this compressed account a little, showing that Nebuzaradan arrived a month after the city's fall (52:12), to take charge of the destruction as well as of the deportation recorded here. The Babylonians needed to keep some balance between reprisals and reconstruction, since chaos would be in no-one's interests: hence the distribution of land to those who could work it (10; cf. 52:16), and the appointment of an acceptable governor (14b, cf. 40:5).

Release for Jeremiah and reassurance for Ebed-melech   39:11–18

As the next chapter will show, Jeremiah had been marched off at first in chains with his fellow captives (40:1), before being set free to join Gedaliah (40:4–6). But such details are of no concern to the present chapter, where the emphasis falls on the complete freedom now given him, guaranteed both by Nebuchadrezzar's instructions and by the number and eminence of the officials made responsible for his release (11–13). From Babylon's point of view, Jeremiah was a loyalist whose good influence should be rewarded and given every opportunity to spread. But behind their action we are to discern the

---

[122] Cf. Lk. 9:24; Jn. 12:25.
[123] Ezk. 17:15.
[124] 34:2–5.

hand of God. This is tacitly implied by the placing of an earlier oracle (15–18) where it is explicitly God alone who determines what shall happen to the man who puts his trust (18b) in him.

As a postscript to the oracle for Ebed-melech, we can notice that it says nothing of the heroism, the compassion or the resourcefulness of his rescue-operation, outstanding though these were: only of the faith in God that was the mainspring of them all. Here, *par excellence*, was the 'faith which worketh by love'.[125]

The prophet's last assignments
40:1 – 44:30

Sadly, the story of Jeremiah's life was to end very much as it had begun, for he had to watch the high promise of a godly leadership – first Josiah's, now Gedaliah's – come to nothing, for lack of any depth of godliness among the rank and file. The prophet whose words had been vindicated to the hilt will bow out still prophesying to the incredulous. Set at liberty by Babylon, he will be last seen carried off by his own people, to end his days not in the promised land but in a land of false gods and broken promises.

False dawn at Mizpah   40:1 – 41:18

Jeremiah joins Gedaliah the new governor   40:1–6

The opening verses give us some details which the summary in 39:11–14 had passed over. The name *Ramah* (1), meaning a 'height', belonged to several places, but the most likely of these would be a town about six miles north of Jerusalem, two or three miles from Mizpah. Notice that Jeremiah, open as ever to a word from the Lord, recognized that word (1a) in the offer of freedom made to him by the captain of the guard, just as he had recognized it in the proposition described in 32:6ff. (see 32:8c). For his response,

[125] Gal. 5:6, AV.

the offer of preferential treatment in Babylon (4) made no appeal to him: everything pointed rather to his staying with Gedaliah (who belonged to a family staunchly sympathetic to him[126]) and with the people whom the Babylonians had not thought worth deporting.

Days of promise   40:7–12

Gedaliah emerges as a peaceable and honourable man, ready for the thankless task of representing the conquering power to his people, and his people to it (10a); meanwhile encouraging a quiet return to normal life. It was a sign of the confidence he inspired, that scattered companies of soldiers with their commanders rallied to him (7–9), soon joined by refugees from all quarters flowing back to the homeland (11–12). The unusually rich yield from vineyards, olive groves and orchards was a further token of God's blessing restored.

A cloud on the horizon   40:13–16

The process of settling down in new conditions, with groups and individuals sorting out their claims on deserted properties,[127] their relations to one another, and their attitudes to a governor whose loyalty to Babylon could be resented, gave a fluid situation in which a power struggle could easily develop. What was Gedaliah to make of the charge against Ishmael (14)? Was he simply a person whom his rivals wanted to eliminate? From our vantage-point we can see that Gedaliah should have enquired of the Lord, whose prophet Jeremiah was with him; yet this is easily said. His mistake did him credit in a way, for it was generous; but it brought his promising regime to an untimely end. It had lasted perhaps as little as two or three months.[128]

Assassination, massacres and abduction   41:1–10

We now learn for the first time that the Ishmael who had taken the

---

[126] Cf. 26:24; 36:10, 11–12, 25, for this family of Shaphan.

[127] Cf. v. 10c: 'your cities that you have taken'.

[128] Cf. 41:1 with 39:2; 52:12. But the year is not named, and 'the seventh month' may be mentioned to explain the presence of pilgrims (41:5) rather than to relate the incident to the events of 587. The influx of home-comers in 40:7–12 is reckoned by some to have needed more time than this.

lead in rallying to Gedaliah with his troops (40:8), but who had come under suspicion (40:13ff.), was of royal descent (1) – hence his bid for power. Everything about him disgraced the name of David his forebear, who had resisted every impulse to 'wade through slaughter to a throne' and had awaited God's time and his people's will.[129] This was no David but a Jehu[130] – and a Jehu without the excuse of a crusade. Almost as outrageous as his treachery was his folly, in supposing that a regime that was devised in deception, imposed by violence, backed by ill-wishers (Ammon, 40:14; 41:10c) and in breach of God's decree (27:6), could have any hope of survival. It may seem far-fetched to draw parallels between this monster and ourselves; but here, although writ large and in blood, is the way in which even the well-meaning may be tempted to get things done, especially in corporate projects. That is, by guile rather than openness; by pressure rather than patience and prayer; in a word, by carnal weapons rather than spiritual, and towards ends of one's own choosing.

Pursuit, rescue and fresh fears   41:11–18

There is irony here, first for Ishmael but then for the rescuers and the rescued. Ishmael finds how delusive is a victory that wins no hearts, as his whole captive company delightedly deserts him (13–14). But the liberated now find themselves alarmingly exposed – free only to face the wrath of Babylon for Gedaliah's murder, while the assassins disappear to take refuge with their Ammonite patrons. In their alarm, the innocent can think only of flight. So, having been spared the long march north to Babylon three months earlier, and now the eastward march to Ammon (10), they instinctively turn south, to gather for a march of their own choosing, into Egypt (17).

Then on second thoughts they wonder if they should enquire what the Lord might have to say ...

False hopes of Egypt   42:1 – 44:30

Divine guidance sought and given   42:1–22

There could hardly be a better plea for guidance than this

---

[129] 1 Sa. 26:10; 2 Sa. 2:1, 4; 5:1
[130] Cf. 2 Ki. 10:12ff.

unanimous (1) and unreserved request (5–6), *that the Lord your God may show us the way we should go, and the thing that we should do* (3). It is a prayer still worth praying daily. Yet a minute flaw on the surface of it, in the words *'your* God', made an admission that went deeper than they realized (despite v.6), as the next chapter will show.

Meanwhile, as once before,[131] we read of Jeremiah waiting patiently for a word from the Lord, rather than producing an immediate and obvious response. Here, *at the end of ten days* (7), the reply was anything but obvious, going clean against the fears and hopes of common sense. But the promise, *I will grant you mercy, that he* (Nebuchadrezzar) *may have mercy on you*, puts in a nutshell the true order of things, the order which we forget when we make faithless and prayerless plans. Equally, the natural view of Egypt as a haven (14) was one that left out the supernatural view of it: that in the circumstances it was not the place that God had chosen for them. In that event, it would prove (as such havens and objectives do) the very opposite of what it promised.

Jeremiah is overridden   43:1–7

If Jeremiah's audience is now speaking of *the Lord our God* (v.2, as against 'the Lord your God' in 42:2), the words are spoken no longer with the fleeting humility of 42:6, but with the arrogance that claims God for their side against Jeremiah. All along (had they realized it) they had regarded God as a power to enlist, not a lord to obey; and they still cannot believe that his will can be radically different from their own. Therefore Jeremiah is lying (his accusers are at least plain-spoken!), and his mentor is not his God but his secretary – perhaps remembered as the one who had made trouble in Jehoiakim's reign by reading out that subversive scroll (36:10).

In gentler terms, the hard sayings of Scripture are still open to attack from both these angles: first, in the name of 'our' version of God (*cf.* 2b), who, we are sure, would never say such things; and then in the assertion that the witnesses who speak in Scripture have listened to other voices than his.

So the prophet is led off once again: not to martyrdom, as he might almost have preferred by now, but to an alien land where his

---

[131] 28:11c–12.

company (apart from the faithful Baruch) would be not pilgrims, nor captives, but deserters.

Egypt will be no refuge   43:8–13

At the very town where the refugees reach at last the safety of Egypt, as they hope,[132] Jeremiah performs this elaborate exercise and speaks this devastating oracle. Not only would the carrying and burying of large stones prolong the mysterious prelude to his words, but the combination of act and speech would signify all the greater certainty of the outcome. Precisely on that spot, in front of the royal residence,[133] Nebuchadrezzar would assert his sovereignty over Egypt, and would be doing so at God's command (10). As for Egypt's impressive temples, gods and obelisks, so reassuring to this superstitious company (as the next chapter reveals them to be), all such things would prove merely combustible, portable or breakable, and the whole land as easily picked up and put on by a conqueror as a cloak by a shepherd (12, NIV, cf. AV).[134]

In the event, Nebuchadrezzar invaded Egypt in 568/7, as a fragmentary Babylonian text records.[135] He left Pharaoh Ahmose (Amasis) on the throne to co-operate with Babylonian policy – hence perhaps the allusion to Egypt's pliability, in the simile of the shepherd's cloak. But we have no details of the campaign.

Jeremiah confronts the refugees   44:1–14

This last encounter between the prophet and his fellow expatriates evidently took place some months or years after their arrival in Egypt, since they were now settled in places far apart, ranging from *Migdol* and *Tahpanhes* at the mouth of the Nile, and *Memphis* (Heb., Noph) just short of the delta, to *the land of Pathros* several hundred miles further upriver. Whether they had gathered for some festival, or whether Jeremiah visited the settlements in turn, the encounter

---

[132] See again their heartfelt words in 42:14.

[133] As a frontier post, Tahpanhes (Daphne to the Greeks) would receive royal visits and would provide a suitable residence. J. Bright (Bright, p. 263) points out that Elephantine, at Egypt's southern frontier, likewise possessed a 'king's house'.

[134] 'As a shepherd wraps his garment round him, so will he wrap Egypt round himself'. The Heb. *'āṭâ* regularly means 'wrap round' (e.g., Ps. 104:2). The suggested alternative, 'de-louse' (cf. RSV, NEB, JB), based on LXX, is needlessly speculative.

[135] ANET, p. 308.

was personal, since we find the remotest of the settlers arguing vigorously with him (15ff.).

The progress from a reasoned survey (leading to the *Therefore...* of v.6), to an impassioned reproach (7–10, *Why...? Why...? Have you forgotten...?*) and finally to judgment (11–14), makes it clear that the wrath of God on the impenitent is as unwelcome to him as it is inevitable. In its thorough, relentless way, this formidable passage is pacing over the ground that our Lord illuminated in a single flash with his outburst in Matthew 23:37–38: 'O Jerusalem, Jerusalem, killing the prophets and stoning those who are sent to you! How often would I have gathered your children together as a hen gathers her brood under her wings, and you would not! Behold, your house is forsaken and desolate.' Incidentally the sweeping judgment on *all ... from the least to the greatest* (12) is characteristically tempered by mercy in the last phrase of the prophecy (14c, *cf.* 28).

The people's choice: the queen of heaven 44:15–30

This is a most revealing glimpse of spiritual perversity – for in blaming all their troubles on the reformation (17–18) instead of on the evils it had tried to root out, these people were turning the truth exactly upside down. Armed with this technique one has an answer – indeed a counter-attack – to everything. Only time would produce its terrible disproof. Then, says the Lord, they *shall know whose word will stand, mine or theirs* (28).

They were to have many successors. At the instinctive level, the fallen mind is always ready to assume that God is the adversary, whom we (like these characters) may blame for our past and distrust for our future. On a more doctrinaire plane, the secularist will blame Christianity, not the lack of it, for many of society's ills, ascribing our frustrations and tensions to the biblical restraints and moral absolutes; seeking freedom, as did Jeremiah's critics, not in God but from God.

A special strength of the queen of heaven's cult was its broad appeal (so enviable a trait of folk religion!), in that it enlisted not only husbands and wives but children in its pleasant routines.[136] But 7:16–20, which describes this family activity, tests it by truth,

---

[136] On 'the queen of heaven' and the cakes made in her honour, see the footnotes to 7:18, p. 50.

not by its trappings. Seen in this light it emerges as in the first place blasphemous and in the long run suicidal.

As for the earthly protector, Pharaoh Hophra (30), he would prove no more of a refuge than poor Zedekiah. He had already shown himself no match for Babylon in his attempt to relieve Jerusalem (37:5–7); and in fact he would eventually lose first his throne (570) and later his life to his relative Ahmose (Amasis), in whose reign Nebuchadrezzar would invade Egypt.[137]

So ends this final confrontation. For the apostates in Egypt the future held nothing; but for their compatriots in Babylon who were accepting their punishment there was the hope of freedom, less than a lifetime away, and the still better prospect of chapters 30 – 33 to follow. Fleeing from God, the refugees had turned their backs on that future.

A possible footnote to their story has come to light in the Elephantine papyri, a fifth-century BC collection of letters and documents belonging to a military colony of Jews settled on an island of the Nile at the then southern frontier of Egypt. A reference to a temple of theirs which had survived a threat of destruction as far back as 525 BC implies that their colony must have been well established at that date – bringing its origin back, if so, to Jeremiah's time or before. Whether its founders were the men of our chapter or another group, it is interesting to note that their cult is revealed as an unblushing mixture of Israelite and Canaanite religion, such as Jeremiah's opponents would have thoroughly appreciated.

Finally, however, the shadow of disaster prophesied by Jeremiah seems to fall across these letters, at least in part, as they tell of recent persecution. In one surviving fragment written by an Egyptian shortly before 400 BC, the writer looks forward to the violent dissolution of this community, which he sees as imminent.[138]

It is worth adding that Egypt was not in itself forbidden territory: it would become an important centre of learning for the later Dispersion, and would shelter the holy family. The sin of Jeremiah's contemporaries was not geographical: it was a vote of no confidence in God.

---

[137] See above, on 43:8–13; and below, on 46:13–24.
[138] Text in, e.g., W. F. Lofthouse, *Israel After the Exile* (*The Clarendon Bible*, IV, Oxford, 1928), p. 230.

Postscript: A remembered message to Baruch 45:1–5

Jeremiah's friend and secretary was taken off to Egypt with him (43:6), burdened now with a special share of opprobrium for his supposed influence over the prophet ('Baruch ... has set you against us', 43:3).

It was a bleak ending to the hopes he had once entertained of *great things for [him]self* (5) – for his family was a distinguished one.[139] But we learn here how he had already faced and agonized over such a cost (3), some twenty years earlier (v.1; *cf.* 36:1, *i.e.*, 605 BC), when he had been called to dare the king's wrath as Jeremiah's spokesman.

God's word to him at that time had been bracing rather than soothing, in much the same way as it had been for the young Jeremiah (*e.g.*, 12:5; 15:19–21). His private drama must not seem hard to him, for there was a bigger tragedy in progress. There is a hint in verse 4 of what it meant to God himself, to be destroying on a vast scale what he had taken care to build and plant; yet with all this he had time for this servant (as he had for the Ethiopian Ebed-melech, 39:15–18), to instruct and reassure and shepherd him.

This little chapter speaks volumes of the 'quick-eyed love', the 'severe mercy' and the 'never-failing providence' of God. What it had to leave unsaid, though it would be a prize even better than the temporary *prize of war* promised to both Baruch and Ebed-melech,[140] was the fact that these two would earn the gratitude of every generation for what they dared to do.[141]

---

[139] His grandfather Maaseiah had been governor of Jerusalem, 32:12; 2 Ch. 34:8.
[140] Je. 39:18; 45:5.
[141] On Jeremiah's friends see Introduction, p. 21, and comments on 36:9–19, p. 120.

PART THREE: Jeremiah 46 – 51
Oracles concerning the nations

Nearly every prophet was given words to speak about the peoples who surrounded ancient Israel – in fact three prophetic books concentrate entirely on a foreign power: Obadiah on Edom, and Jonah and Nahum on Nineveh. If we needed convincing that the God of Israel was seen as Lord of the whole earth, here would be proof enough.

The humbling of Egypt   46:1–28

Egypt and the battle of Carchemish   46:1–12

The name Carchemish (2) introduces us to one of the decisive battles of world history, fought in 605 BC (*the fourth year of Jehoiakim*, 2). Seven years earlier, in 612, the great Assyrian empire had had its death blow in the destruction of its capital, Nineveh, leaving the powers of east and west to fight it out for the succession. On the route between Babylon and Egypt, Carchemish (*in the north by the river Euphrates*, 6b) made the natural confrontation point; and it was on his way there that Pharaoh Neco had slain King Josiah of Judah in 609 when Josiah tried to turn him back.[1] For the next four years the Egyptian army was based on Carchemish, and Pharaoh dominated Syria and Palestine,[2] setting up his puppet-kings while Babylon's main force was preoccupied elsewhere. Then at last the Babylonian army fell upon the Egyptians in 605, routing them utterly.

The ballad is brilliant, first capturing the excitement of the action (3–6), then singing of the vaulting ambition that God has brought low (7–12). In the opening scene we hear the rapid orders to the foot-soldiers and the cavalry as they bustle to get equipped and positioned (3–4) – then we watch, amazed (*Why ...?*, 5), the anticlimax of total, scrambling, unavailing flight. It is their turn now for Jeremiah's refrain, *terror on every side* (5).[3]

The taunt-song of verses 7–12 dwells on the theme which David epitomized in his lament for Saul, 'How are the mighty fallen!' The mood is a mixture of triumph and pathos as one contemplates the disastrous folly of a false idea of glory, exposed at last for what it is. To emulate the Nile in its great surge beyond its banks, and to outdo it by a bid to submerge the whole world for Egypt (7–8), was a majestic metaphor, but it had overlooked the difference between an inundation that brought life and one that gloried in destruction.

> *He said, I will rise, I will cover the earth,*
> *I will destroy cities and their inhabitants* (8).

So the bombast of verse 9, boasting of the famous chariot force[4] and of the host of mercenaries,[5] propelled Egypt not to a day of victory but to the day of the Lord (10):

> *For the Lord God of hosts holds a sacrifice*
> *in the north country by the river Euphrates.*

But once again Jeremiah is shown a nation's plight not merely in

[1] 2 Ch. 35:20ff.

[2] *Cf.* 2 Ch. 36:1–4; 2 Ki. 23:31–35.

[3] See the references at 6:25, p. 47, footnote.

[4] *Cf.* Is. 31:1, 3

[5] 'Put' (9) may be Punt, at the southern end of the Red Sea. The Ludim seem unlikely to be the Lydians of Asia Minor, and may be an error for the 'Lubim', or Libyans, who are coupled with the men of Ethiopia and Put as allies of Egypt in Na. 3:9.

terms of eternal disaster, but of a sickness beyond natural remedy (11). He speaks of his own people in such terms (8:22; 30:12), and likewise of Babylon (51:8). Above all, he has faced the universal disorder of the human heart (17:9), not excluding his own, and has cried for healing (17:14). He has every right to be God's spokesman on the theme.

Egypt awaiting invasion   46:13–24

After her rout at Carchemish and the inevitable loss of Syria and Palestine to Nebuchadrezzar, Egypt might well have found herself on the conqueror's list. As things turned out, however, as far as we know it was not until 568/7 that the blow fell – and fell with moderation. But this oracle left no doubt of Egypt's helplessness in face of anything the enemy might do.

The place-names in verse 14 are of the frontier towns in the path of an invader from the north-east, together with Memphis the capital of Lower (*i.e.* northern) Egypt. But the call to make a stand there only emphasizes how frail is her defence, with evidently her boasted mercenaries of verse 9 (*cf.* v.21) melting away to their *own people* and their homelands (16).[6]

The poem is alive with descriptive touches: the towering conqueror (like mount Tabor dominating the surrounding plain, or like Carmel's massive promontory, 18); the prize herd stampeding (20–21); the serpent slithering away (22); the crashing forest; the locust swarm (23). Above all there is the devastating summing-up of Pharaoh in verse 17 as *Noisy one who lets the hour go by* (to which we might respond, 'Lord, is it I?'). NEB puts it pungently: 'King Bombast, the man who missed his moment' – making him a fit monarch for the Egypt which Isaiah had dismissed as 'Dragon Do-nothing' (Is. 30:7, Moffatt).[7]

Egypt's distant gleam of light   46:25–26

This postscript, before it can speak of mercy, must reaffirm the fate of all that is false or that trusts in falsehood, adding now Amon the god of Thebes, capital of Upper Egypt, to the probable mention of

---

[6] Probably, too, she is taunted for Apis, the futile bull-god of Memphis (so RSV and most modern versions, following LXX).

[7] See also on 44:30, p. 134.

Apis the god of Memphis in verse 15. Whether or not the Egyptians heard these prophecies, the idolatrous refugees from Judah will certainly have done so, and will have needed them.

At last the horizon brightens for Egypt (26b), as it will for others of these nations;[8] and we may remember that the prophecy of 12:14ff. goes further still, to offer spiritual blessings as well as material to any who are teachable. If we want an even brighter prophecy for Egypt, Isaiah 19:19–25 vies with Psalm 87:4[9] in the lengths to which it goes.

Light for Jacob too   46:27–28

These two verses have met us already at 30:10–11, following a promise of the Messiah ('David their king', 30:9), and there are comments there (p. 104). What is rather touching about their position here, is the evident concern (of Baruch, as editor?) to remind an Israel now under a cloud that if there is a future for even Egypt after its ordeal (26b), how much more can God's covenant people be certain of his fairness (*in just measure*, 28b), and of the grace that he delights in.

The sword of the Lord against the Philistines   47:1–7

We know too little of the times to be sure when it was that *Pharaoh smote Gaza* (1). Possibly it was while Pharaoh Neco was in *the north* (2) between 609 and 605, awaiting his trial of strength with Nebuchadrezzar on the Euphrates, and asserting meanwhile his

---

[8] See 48:47; 49:6, 39.

[9] Still using (now affectionately?) the 'monster' nickname Rahab, as in Is. 30:7!

power over Palestine.[10] If so, the *waters ... rising out of the north* would soon be overtaken by the *overflowing torrent* (2) of the Babylonians as they swept all before them after overwhelming the Egyptians at Carchemish.[11] A Babylonian prism, now in Istanbul, mentions the presence – presumably with little choice in the matter – of the kings of Tyre and Sidon (*cf.* v.4), of Gaza (5) and of Ashdod, at the court of Nebuchadrezzar; while a prison list now in Berlin records the rations for the king of Ashkelon (5), among other noted prisoners (including Jehoiachin of Judah).[12]

The poem has its vivid touches of sound (3a) and sight, most poignantly in the glimpse of the battle-shocked (3b). But verses 6 and 7 stand out, with their desperate, unavailing protest,

> *Ah, sword of the Lord!*
> *How long till you are quiet?*

If we are still echoing it to this day, we must accept the same reply, in which there is nothing arbitrary – nothing, that is, except the arbitrariness of our human state of mutiny. While that persists, *How can it be quiet ...?*

Tears for Moab   48:1–47

Moab, whose high tableland on the far side of the Dead Sea had formed the eastern skyline for Jeremiah from his youth, had ties of kinship with Israel, not only through Lot but through Ruth the ancestress of David. It was a bitter enemy as often as not, and its god Chemosh (7, 13, 46) an affront to the Lord; yet its place-names

---

[10] See the opening comments on 46:1–12.

[11] The pursuit of the Egyptians was interrupted in 605 by news of the death of Nebuchadrezzar's father, King Nabopolassar, upon which Nebuchadrezzar returned to Babylon to ascend the throne. But the campaign was soon resumed, and the Babylonian Chronicle records the sack of Ashkelon in 604 (v. 5).

[12] For extracts from both lists see *ANET*, p. 308.

(abundant in this chapter – see especially vv. 21–24) were as familiar to Israelites as their own. The thought of aliens trampling its cities and its pastures (8) was as grievous to Jeremiah, and to Isaiah before him,[13] as to the Lord.

But, grievous or not, judgment had to fall. The picture of Moab that builds up in the chapter is, above all, one of arrogance. 'We have heard of the pride of Moab', said Isaiah long before (Is. 16:6), and Jeremiah now repeats it (29), for nothing has changed. To us at this distance the very mention of her *renown* (2a) is ironic, for we can see how local and how temporary was the fame that meant so much to her (*cf.*, for reflection, Je. 9:23–24; Jn. 12:43). With hindsight, too, we can see what verse 7 viewed with foresight, namely the frailty of man's best defences and reserves. For defence, Moab had towering cliffs, and for wealth, her enormous flocks of sheep;[14] riches that were self-renewing. But the shelter of these things had bred more complacency than character. In some famous lines, verse 11 makes it clear that to be undisturbed may be better treatment for a wine than for a nation: that (as we might say) to be mellow and full-bodied is the wrong excellence to aspire to!

> *Moab has been at ease from his youth*
> *and has settled on his lees;*[15]
> *he has not been emptied from vessel to vessel,*
> *nor has he gone into exile;*
> *so his taste remains in him,*
> *and his scent is not changed* (11).

Readers of the missionary classic, *Hudson Taylor in Early Years*,[16] may remember the apt heading, 'Emptied from Vessel to Vessel', to a chapter describing an unsettled but ultimately fruitful few months in the missionary's second year in China. Nothing fruitful, however, is promised for a Moab which has *magnified himself against the Lord* (26, reiterated in v.42): only disillusion within (13) and derision without (vv.26–27, 39).

In passing, note the fearful twist to what may well have been a proverb or a preacher's text in verse 10a (*Cursed is he who does the work*

[13] *Cf.* esp. Is. 15:5–6 ('My heart cries out for Moab …'); 16:9–11, with Je. 48:5, 31–36.

[14] *Cf.* the huge figures of 2 Ki. 3:4. For a fine study of the whole region, see D. Baly, *The Geography of the Bible* (Lutterworth, 1957), ch. 19: 'Ammon, Moab and Edom'.

[15] *Cf.* Is. 25:6.

[16] By Dr and Mrs Howard Taylor (CIM, 1911). The chapter is XXIV.

of the Lord with slackness), turning it into a charge to Moab's executioners. It chimes in with the note of unsparing judgment which coexists in the chapter with the note of grief (see, *e.g.*, vv.17, 31, 32, 36, for the latter). On the relation between these apparent incompatibles, see the comment on the closing verses of chapter 47.

Yet, in the distant future, there was to be renewal for Moab (47), as there would also be for Egypt and some others.[17] This surprising sequel illuminates the saying that 'mercy triumphs over judgment' (Jas. 2:13b); yet the silence of companion passages (49:7–33) forbids us to take mercy for granted (*cf.*, *e.g.*, Jas. 2:13a). An old comment on the penitent and the impenitent thief at Calvary is apposite: 'One was saved, that none might despair; yet only one, that none might presume.'

Ammon dispossessed   49:1–6

When Reuben and Gad got permission to settle on the far side of the Jordan,[18] they were storing up trouble for themselves: Reuben with the Moabites to the south of them, and Gad with Ammon to the east. Territory kept changing hands as fortunes waxed and waned, but Reuben eventually disintegrated,[19] and Gad was deported by Assyria in 734/3,[20] leaving its land open to the Ammonites (1).

Baalis, king of Ammon, was to deal a disastrous blow against Judah by instigating the murder of Gedaliah (40:14; 41:15). But the prophecy fastens upon a far more sinister 'king': the god Milcom (1, 3).[21] Better known to us as Molech, he had been worshipped here with rites of child-sacrifice since before the days of Moses. The mention of this god as the invader at the head of his people (1) puts the matter on a plane above the political. His cult had always been denounced with special horror (*e.g.*, Dt. 12:31), and was itself

---

[17] See the references at 46:26b.

[18] Nu. 32.

[19] See, *e.g.*, the place-names in Reuben's inheritance (Jos. 13:15–23) which reappear as Moabite possessions in Is. 15 – 16 and Je. 48.

[20] 2 Ki. 15:29 ('Gilead').

[21] See the footnotes to 19:5, p. 79.

invasive, especially in times of crisis when some desperate cultic act seemed called for;[22] therefore there was more than territory involved in the promise that *Israel shall dispossess those who dispossessed him* (2).

Long before the return of this region to Jewish hands,[23] Ammon was to be in trouble: first through Nebuchadrezzar's reprisals in 582 for Gedaliah's murder,[24] and soon afterwards, fatally, through a wave of invasions from the Arabian desert, by tribes which overran not only her but Moab and Edom. By the end of the century all three peoples had been driven out, and their territories taken over.[25]

On the prospect of ultimate mercy (6), the last such promise till verse 39, see the remarks on 48:47.

Edom stripped bare   49:7–22

Much of verses 7–16 runs parallel with Obadiah, sometimes almost word for word, although the order is different[26] and each prophet has also his own unshared material in this opening section. Then they part company in verses 17–22, some of whose verses (19–21) will provide words for not only Edom's calamity but Babylon's as well (50:44–46).

Edom was evidently well known for two great assets: her wise men and her almost inaccessible strongholds. The former seem implied by verse 7 and Obadiah 8,[27] and the latter are exemplified by Petra (probably 'the rock', Sela, of v. 16),[28] whose only approach is through a tortuous and narrow defile, and by Bozrah, which is perched, eagle-like, on its rocky height (*cf.* 16b).

---

[22] *Cf.* 7:31; 32:35; 2 Ki. 16:3; Zp. 1:5.

[23] The Maccabean Jonathan seems to have been granted it ('Perea') in 144 BC.

[24] Josephus, *Antiquities*, X.ix.7. *Cf.* Je. 52:30.

[25] See, *e.g.*, Bright, pp. 323, 327, 332.

[26] *E.g.*, Ob. 1–4 corresponds with our vv. 14–16, and Ob. 5–6 with our 9–10a.

[27] Job's learned friend Eliphaz was from Teman (Jb. 2:11).

[28] D. Baly, however, identifies Sela as the stronghold on the height Umm el-Biyara in the centre of Petra (D. Baly, *The Geography of the Bible*, p. 245).

To a people more used to inspiring fear than experiencing it (16a), God speaks of total disaster:

> *If grape-gatherers came to you,*
> *would they not leave gleanings?*
> *... But I have stripped Esau bare*
> *... and he is no more* (9–10).

So it was to happen. Within a century, the Arabian tribes that overran Moab and Ammon would have driven the Edomites out of their land into the south of Judah; and these invaders would be replaced in turn by the powerful kingdom of the Nabateans.

Verse 12 raises the question of relative guilt and innocence. *Those who did not deserve to drink the cup* might seem at first sight to be a reference to Judah; but with the whole book contradicting such a thought the allusion must be to the incidental suffering brought upon those who simply happened to lie on an invader's path. Edom's guilt is treated here as self-evident, but is not specified. It is left to other scriptures to tell of her undying hatred towards Israel (Am. 1:11) – so unlike the magnanimity of Esau in Genesis 33:4ff. – a hatred manifested from the time of Moses right on to the Babylonian capture of Jerusalem, when Edom not only gloated over its fall but looted it and cut off its fugitives.[29] In Isaiah 34 this reprobate brother-nation to Israel is pictured as receiving the full force of the world's judgment day, standing over against Zion as the profane to the sacred, somewhat as Babylon stands over against the city of God in the closing chapters of Revelation.

Damascus in panic   49:23–27

From Edom in the far south we turn to Syria at the opposite extreme, moving north from Damascus to the petty kingdoms of Hamath (opposite Cyprus) and Arpad (beyond Aleppo, towards

---

[29] Nu. 20:14–21; Ps. 137:7; Ezk. 25:12–14; Ob. 11–14.

Carchemish). A century-and-a-half before, these had suffered from being on the Assyrians' invasion route to Palestine; and evidently they went through the same ordeal again when the battle of Carchemish opened the floodgates to Nebuchadrezzar.

The cry, *How ...!* (25) opens many a lament in Scripture, and many a taunt,[30] as it exclaims over the fallen fortunes of small and great. Often there are mixed feelings, even over a well-deserved disaster – as when Moab's fall is lamented in 48:20 and derided in 48:39. Here likewise there is a sense of tragedy at the blighting of joy and youth (25–26), yet also a quiet indication that the blow was due and overdue, by the allusion in verse 27 to an earlier prophet's warnings.[31] The mills of God grind slowly ...!

The tents of Kedar in affliction   49:28–33

Not even the elusive desert-dwellers would be beyond the reach of Nebuchadrezzar when God saw fit to send him. His own motive (30b) would be doubtless to assert his authority, for these tribes of the eastern desert[32] were a threat to their settled neighbours, who were now part of his empire. The Assyrian king Asshurbanipal had had trouble with them in the previous century (*ANET*, p. 297), and the Babylonian Chronicle records an expedition (this one?) against them in 599/8.

The call to them in verse 30, as to Edom in verse 8, to 'dwell deep' (AV) has understandably attracted preachers by its devotional sound; but in its context it is advice to take to the depths of the desert, since their free and carefree way of life is threatened. *A nation at ease, that dwells securely, ... that dwells alone* (31) may remind us of the self-satisfied Moab of 48:11 and 29, or even of the rich fool (Lk 12:13–21), but it is also a witness to the precariousness of all human reckonings. The saying, 'It can never happen here', is only true, we are reminded, without its middle word.

[30] *E.g.*, 2 Sa. 1:19; Is. 14:4, 12; Je. 48:17, 39; La. 1:1; 2:1; 4:1.
[31] Am. 1:3–5, esp. v. 4.
[32] Kedar was an Ishmaelite tribe (Gn. 25:13, 16). The Hazor (*ḥāṣôr*) of these verses was not

The bow of Elam broken   49:34–39

Elam, an ancient kingdom at the head of the Persian Gulf, was the most distant of the peoples addressed in these oracles: a trading nation of wealth and, intermittently, of military power until its crushing defeat by the Assyrian Asshurbanipal in 640, when it ceased to be a kingdom. Part of its scattering (36) began then, and Ezra 4:9–10 mentions the deporting of 'the men of Susa, that is, the Elamites' to Samaria by 'the great and noble Osnappar', *i.e.*, Asshurbanipal.[33] When Persia rose to power, from *c.*550, Elam became merely one of its satrapies, and Susa the winter residence of the Persian kings. (Is v. 38 an allusion to this, since imperial rulers are God's puppet-kings? *Cf.* the language of, *e.g.*, Je. 27:6; Is. 44:28 – 45:7.)

As with the other prophecies here, and indeed with God's message to mankind, verse 35 singles out *the mainstay of their might* for his special attention. Elam relied on its archers (35; *cf.* Is. 22:6), Ammon on its Molech (Milcom, v. 3), Edom on its cleverness and its crags (vv. 7, 16), Damascus on its fame (25), Kedar on its remoteness and its mobility (29, 31). The list could be extended and modernized, or it could be summed up in the great saying of 9:23–24:

> Let not the wise man glory in his wisdom, ...
> the mighty man ... in his might, ...
> the rich man ... in his riches;
> but let him who glories glory in this,
> that he understands and knows me ...

Then grace breaks through for Elam (39), as for others.[34] The movements of peoples over the millennia make their fortunes hard to trace, but the curtain lifts an inch or two on the day of Pentecost,

---

the walled city in north Palestine but either a desert settlement or, as Bright suggests (Bright, p. 336), possibly a collective term for the *haṣērîm* or unwalled villages (*cf.* v. 31; Gn. 25:16) of these tribes.

[33] Under the same Assyrian policy of disintegrating the defeated (*cf.* 2 Ki. 17:24), there were Israelites deported to Elam: *cf.* Is. 11:11.

[34] See the references at 46:26b.

when Elamites were found to be among the multitude who heard of 'the wonderful works of God' in their own tongue.[35]

The doom of Babylon   50:1 – 51:64

Fittingly, the empire which struck the most devastating blow ever suffered by the kingdom of David, receives the longest series of oracles about her own future.

Two things challenge us to relate what is said here to what we learn elsewhere, both in other scriptures and in the events of history. First, there is the fact that the Babylon condemned in these chapters is the same Babylon whose yoke (said God) was to be accepted until her time should come – and accepted with a good grace.[36] At the same time, her role as God's unwitting *hammer and weapon of war*,[37] as she wantonly pursued her own ends,[38] would give her no escape from justice. So retribution dominates these oracles; but it awaits God's time and agents. The instruction to 'seek the welfare' of the conquering city (29:7) is not revoked: there is no call to revolution.

Secondly, there is a problem of interpretation, in that the fall of Babylon which ended Judah's exile in 539 happened without a battle. The city was not attacked by *a company of great nations* who would *come against her from every quarter; open her granaries; pile her up like heaps of grain, and destroy her utterly*;[39] nor did God's people have to flee for their lives.[40] When Cyrus entered, it was as a liberator, to a city intact and welcoming. Half a century later, Xerxes would put down a rebellion there with a heavy hand, smashing its fortifications and pillaging its temples; but the city survived and recovered. Its

---

[35] Acts 2:9, 11, av.
[36] Chapters 27 – 29; esp. 27:5–15; 29:7.
[37] 51:20ff., *cf.* Is. 10:5–7, 15.
[38] 50:11ff.
[39] 50:9, 26.
[40] *Cf.* 51:6, 45.

eventual decline into *a heap of ruins* (51:37), *a wilderness dry and desert* (50:12b), was gradual, due largely to the building of a new capital, Seleucia on the Tigris, in 275 BC; but it still had inhabitants in the first century AD.

Two scriptures, Jeremiah 18 and Revelation 17 – 18, may throw light on this. In Jeremiah 18:7–8 we have already noted the words: 'If at any time I declare concerning a nation or a kingdom, that I will pluck up and break down and destroy it, and if that nation ... turns from its evil, I will repent of the evil that I intended to do to it.' It is at least possible that the humbling of Nebuchadrezzar, culminating in his testimony in Daniel 4:34–37, opened the door to the mercy of 539 – for it is obvious from God's generous response to even an Ahab, a Manasseh, or the city of Nineveh, that he meets a change of attitude more than halfway.[41]

The other scripture, Revelation 17 –18, opens our eyes to another dimension of the Babylon of these chapters: as the embodiment of this world's corrupt power and glory, and the archetypal opposite of Zion the city of God. That passage borrows directly from these oracles, speaking of the *golden cup* with which she makes the nations drunk;[42] of her judgment reaching up to heaven;[43] of her fall, to rise no more;[44] summoning God's people to flee from the midst of her, lest they share her punishment.[45] In this capacity, the Babylon of these visions will have no gentle downfall, but one as catastrophic as anything that the language of ancient warfare can depict.

In the notes that follow, only a few details within this broad picture will be taken up.

'They shall ask the way to Zion'   *50:1–10*

The phrase, *In those days* (4), is nearly always a pointer to the messianic age to come. The vision of a reunited and converted people, joined to the Lord in an everlasting covenant, looks beyond the 'day of small things'[46] which followed the return from exile, to the gospel age and beyond, as depicted in ch. 31 and in 32:36ff.

---

[41] See 1 Ki. 21:27–29; 2 Ch. 33:10–13; Jon. 3:10.
[42] Je. 51:7; Rev. 17:2, 4.
[43] Je. 51:9; Rev. 18:5 (her sins).
[44] Je. 51:63–64; Rev. 18:21.
[45] Je. 50:8; 51:6; Rev. 18:4.
[46] Zc. 4:10.

'Do to her as she has done' 50:11–16

This is a call, not to Israel but to the attacking armies who will be the agents of divine retribution (a more objective word than *vengeance*, 15b). This emphasis on deserved punishment is prominent;[47] but see what is said above on the mercy shown to the historical Babylon, in contrast to the final judgment on her spiritual counterpart.

Pasture without predators 50:17–20

Verse 6 spoke of 'lost sheep', badly shepherded;[48] and the more violent scenes of verse 17 could be its natural sequel. Politically, the intrigues and treacheries of Judah's kings ('shepherds', as the Old Testament regards them) had brought Assyria and now Babylon to the kill. Spiritually too (to adopt the New Testament connotation of 'shepherd'), a badly pastored flock is soon astray, then swiftly preyed upon.

After that violent opening, the picture of lush pastures (19) and then the straight promise of a transformed and pardoned people (20), brings out the miraculous nature of the change that God intends. It is the New Covenant, no less;[49] and whether the delightful language of verse 20 expresses what we know as justification, or leaps ahead to our resurrection and sinless state, either way it is our inheritance.

'Come against her from every quarter' 50:21–40

Changes of speed and rhythm vary the attack: notice especially the staccato incisiveness of *A sword ... A sword ...* in verses 35–38, over against the rolling lines of, *e.g.*, verses 21–27 (themselves far from uniform). Notice too the rapid changes of stance: summoning the invaders,[50] surveying the overthrow,[51] addressing the tyrant,[52] heartening the captives.[53]

---

[47] *Cf.* vv. 18, 29; 51:6, 9, 11.
[48] *Cf.* 23:1–4; Ezk. 34.
[49] *Cf.* 31:33–34.
[50] *E.g.*, vv. 21, 26–27, 29, 35–38
[51] Vv. 22–23, 39–40.
[52] Vv. 24, 31–32.
[53] Vv. 28, 33–34.

On a point of detail, commentators have drawn attention to the word-play in verse 21, where Marratim and Puqudu[54] become *Merathaim* ('double rebellion') and *Pekod* ('punishment'). The prophets were fond of giving a word this kind of twist, adding to the liveliness of an attack and fastening it in the memory. (Preachers, please note!)

Babylon's turn now 50:41–46

The special interest of these two short oracles lies in the fact that they have been employed already against two different targets: verses 41–43 substantially against Zion itself (6:22–24), and verses 40, 44–46 against Edom (49:18–21). The force of this is surely first the irony of Babylon's being no longer the menace from the north (41) but the one menaced now from there; and secondly the humbling fact that in the end there is little to choose between what awaits the pride of an empire and the pride of a clan – the only difference being in the reverberations of their respective falls (compare that of Edom, 'heard at the Red Sea', 49:21, with that of Babylon, *heard among the nations*, 50:46).

'We would have healed Babylon, but ...' 51:1–10

Here, in verses 6–10, is the seminal picture of Babylon as the metropolis of evil and the seducer of mankind which will be elaborated in Revelation 17 – 18 (see above, p. 149). What is special to this passage is the note of sadness over her incurable condition (8b–9a) – a note which chimes in with this book's description of sin as desperate sickness,[55] and also with the many glimpses of God's reluctant resort to judgment when all else has failed.[56]

In passing, note the irony of verse 9b: that man's attempt to build himself up to the skies ends only in building up his judgment (*cf.* also Rev. 18:5). The allusion to the tower of Babel is blurred for us by the convention that we call Babel 'Babylon' wherever it occurs in the Old Testament after Genesis 11:9. 'Babylon' is the Greek (and therefore the New Testament's) form of the name.

---

[54] Respectively, a district and a people of Babylonia, chosen here perhaps for their punning possibilities.

[55] See the reference and comments at 46:11, p. 138f.

[56] See the comments on ch. 48.

'Vengeance for his temple' 51:11–14

When God scorned the superstitious parrot-cry, 'The temple of the Lord' (7:4), and gave notice of that building's destruction, he was not belittling his house, nor exonerating its desecrators. Psalm 74 recalls the savage shouts with which they went to work:

> Your foes roared in the place where you met with us,
>> they set up their standards as signs ...
> They smashed all the carved panelling
>> with their axes and hatchets.
> They burned your sanctuary to the ground;
>> they defiled the dwelling-place of your Name
>>> (Ps. 74:4, 6–7, NIV)

– and the thoroughness of it made the intention clear: to make the temple not only physically but ritually unusable. It was, to their minds, a crippling blow against the God of Israel.

To that fantasy God replies in verses 11–14, within which the quietest line is perhaps the most devastating (13b):

> *your end has come,*
>> *the thread of your life is cut.*[57]

In view of the larger connotation of 'Babylon' in Revelation 17 – 18, we are reminded that the world's campaign against God's living temple is equally ill-fated, its rejoicing premature,[58] and its life-span predetermined.

The one and only God 51:15–19

Against the arrogance of mere men, and the pretensions of mere idols, this poem is magnificently dismissive. It is also entirely assured of the paradox that the Creator and little Israel are everything to one another: the Creator as Israel's *portion*, and Israel as his *inheritance* (19).

The irony of the passage, nevertheless, is that originally these words had had to be addressed not to the heathen in their blindness but to Israel in its perversity (*cf.* 10:12–16, word for word).

---

[57] Lit., 'the cubit [*i.e.*, the measure] of your cutting off ' – a figure taken from weaving, when the work has reached its due length and is cut off from the loom; *cf.* Is. 38:12b. This terse phrase, however, can alternatively be translated, '... the measure of your gain', *cf.* AV.

[58] *Cf.* Rev. 11:1–19, esp. vv. 10ff.

War club and volcano 51:20–26

Unlike the sledge-hammer of 50:23 and 23:29, this shatterer is a weapon rather than a tool. Everything here stresses the indiscriminate ruin that an aggressor spreads around him, whatever his military objectives; yet God is using this cruel instrument before he breaks it. Isaiah 10:5ff. points out the gulf between the aggressor's motives and the Lord's, and promises retribution on him (Assyria) as does our verse 24 on Babylon. But our passage faces us with the mystery of what God allows, especially in verses 22–23, and gives us no encouragement to probe it. Other scriptures assure us of a final judgment where nothing will be dealt out indiscriminately,[59] and of a present providence whereby nothing is meaningless;[60] but here the interest is strictly confined to Babylon: its role and its requital.

So the picture changes from Babylon as a weapon to Babylon as a *destroying mountain* (25–26) – in fact, as a volcano which not only spews out destruction but ends by blowing itself to bits. Once again the Babylon which is the city of man looms up behind the local power-base, doomed as she was doomed. 'The world passes away, and the lust of it', together with the earth itself in the day of the Lord, 'burned up' like the destroying mountain of this passage.[61] It is no object to give one's heart to.[62]

Empire against empire 51:27–33

From metaphor we turn to realism: from a mountain on fire to a city invaded. The three kingdoms of verse 27, all within Armenia, were part of the empire of the Medes (28), which spread in a great arc to the north of Babylon's dominions. When Cyrus took over that empire he first extended it westward to the Aegean, to absorb the rich kingdom of King Croesus of Lydia (547/6); then, it seems, eastward to Afghanistan and beyond. In *c.* 540 he was ready to descend on Babylon after annexing much of its empire. Something of the *trembling* (29) induced by his approach is reflected in Isaiah 41:1–7 (esp. v. 5), where the dismay of the heathen is contrasted with the calm assertion that the Lord is directing these events towards the liberation of Israel.[63]

[59] Rev. 20:12.
[61] 1 Jn. 2:17; 2 Pet. 3:10.
[63] *Cf.* Is. 44:28 – 45:7.

[60] *E.g.*, Is. 45:5–7; 46:8–10.
[62] *Cf.* 1 Jn. 2:15, Phillips.

It is difficult to be sure whether the prophecy here is of a violent overthrow which, in the event, God modified in mercy (see the discussion above, introducing chs. 50 – 51, pp. 148ff.), or whether the unopposed capture of the city did include some burning of buildings as in verses 30c, 32. There is no reference to slaughter in this passage: only to warriors who offer no fight (30, 32) and to messengers running hither and thither with news of the coup (31).

According to Herodotus, 'owing to the great size of the city the outskirts were captured without the people in the centre knowing anything about it: there was a festival going on,[64] and they continued to dance and enjoy themselves, until they learned the news the hard way'.[65]

'He has swallowed me like a monster' 51:34–44

Usually, though not invariably, the Hebrew word *tannîn* (34) means a sea or river monster, as in Genesis 1:21; and we may well be meant to see Israel pictured as sharing Jonah's predicament and rescue.

> *Nebuchadrezzar ... has swallowed me like a monster ...* (34)
> *... And I* (the Lord) *will punish Bel in Babylon.*
> *and take out of his mouth what he has swallowed* (44).

Whether as sea monster or as dragon, Babylon is embodied here first in her king, whose potency created her empire; and then in one of her chief gods, whose *im*potence was proclaimed in 50:2 and put mercilessly on show in Isaiah 46:1–2.

Between these two pictures, of Israel successively swallowed and disgorged, there is a riot of word painting, some literal (as in vv. 36–37, where the drying up of the great reservoir (*the sea*) of Queen Nitocris[66] and of the wells and irrigation system have reduced Babylon to barrenness), and some highly figurative. The two are side by side in verses 42–43, with none of our literary inhibitions over combining a metaphorical sea with a literal desert.

Once again, as in 50:23, the theme of 'How are the mighty

---

[64] *Cf.* Dn. 5:1, 30.
[65] Herodotus, *The Histories*, I, 191 (Translated by A. de Sélincourt, Penguin Classics, ²1972, p. 118).
[66] Herodotus, *The Histories*, I, 185 (p. 115, Penguin edn.).

fallen!' meets us in verse 41[67] over the fall of Babylon,[68] lest we fail to take to heart the transience of earthly fame. From being *the praise of the whole earth* to becoming *a horror* (41) or simply a spent force, a place to which *the nations shall no longer flow* (44), is no unusual sequence, given time enough. So passes the world's glory.

This is no place for God's people   51:45–51

As in verses 6–10, there are themes here which will reappear in Revelation 18 concerning the spiritual Babylon, the 'City of Destruction' as *Pilgrim's Progress* was to call it. *Go out of the midst of her*[69] is a call which reflects this city's hold upon even those whose true home is elsewhere – a fact underlined by the outspoken verse 50:

> *Remember the Lord from afar,*
> *and let Jerusalem come into your mind.*

Like the sons-in-law of Lot in Sodom, many of the exiles in Babylon preferred to stay on when Jerusalem beckoned them through Cyrus's decree of liberty in 538. Like the reluctant Christian, they did well out of their choice in worldly terms, for Babylon comfortably outlasted them. Even its destruction by Xerxes, half a century later (*c.*485) was not its death blow, for like its greater equivalent it had great staying power. But God looks on to the last Act: ... *behold, the days are coming* ... (47). That final moment is decreed here in the words, *Babylon must fall* (49), to be echoed in the angel's proclamation of Revelation 18:2, 'Fallen, fallen is Babylon the great!' As in our chapter (51:48), so in Revelation 18:20, this is greeted with the joy that is evoked by long-awaited justice – although the latter passage picks up the sound of weeping from those who have shared her affluence and now confront their ruin.[70]

'For the Lord is a God of recompense'   51:52–58

Retribution (56), as we have seen,[71] looms large in these chapters,

[67] See the comments at 46:7–12 (p. 138) on the mixed emotions of these 'How' sayings.
[68] The code-name *šešak* is used in 41a for Babel (Babylon). See note on p. 95.
[69] v. 45, *cf.* Rev. 18:4.
[70] Rev. 18:9–19 draws on the oracle of Ezk. 27 against Tyre, the trading city which portrays the power and the allure of wealth, whereby 'bodies and souls of men' come to be counted as so much merchandise (Rev. 18:13, NIV, *cf.* Ezk. 27:13).
[71] See on 50:11–16.

and is seen here as especially the answer to hubris, that is, to the pretensions of false religion (52) and human arrogance (53) — that pride which had classically overreached itself in the tower of Babel and which had never been renounced in the Babylon of any era. So the city's invaders will be as relentless as a tidal wave, her protectors as useless as the drugged, and her defences *levelled to the ground* (58).

In the last words of this oracle (58b) we stand back to ask, in effect, what this vaulting ambition of the few and the jostling struggle of the many amounts to in the end. The answer is borrowed from Habakkuk 2:13:

> The peoples labour for naught,
>   and the nations weary themselves only for fire.

In Habakkuk, where God is answering a question about the sufferings of the righteous, the saying goes on to add (Hab. 2:14):

> For the earth will be filled
>   with the knowledge of the glory of the Lord,
>   as the waters cover the sea.

But Babylon, as the kingdom of man, has no part in that prospect. It has spent itself 'only for fire'.

'Thus shall Babylon sink' 51:59–64

The fourth year of Zedekiah (59) was also the fourth year of the 597 captivity, in which Jeconiah (Jehoiachin) and the leading citizens of Judah had been deported. Zedekiah's summons to Babylon was doubtless to make sure of his loyalty, perhaps in view of reports that envoys of five neighbouring states had been conferring with him at Jerusalem.[72]

Seraiah, as the brother of Baruch, was a man Jeremiah could trust with a task of some danger, although the reading of the scroll did not have to be in public. The words spoken and then acted out would set in motion the curse on Babylon; and the symbolic action would be repeated still more impressively in John's vision of the Babylon of the Apocalypse:

---

[72] See 27:1ff., and for the date, 28:1. Possibly, however, the meeting at Jerusalem followed his return from Babylon.

Then a mighty angel took up a stone like a great millstone and
threw it into the sea, saying,

> 'So shall Babylon the great city be thrown down
>   with violence,
> and shall be found no more.[73]

In the order of the book as we have it, with only the historical
appendix to follow, there is a fitting finality in the note: *Thus far are
the words of Jeremiah*. For the people of God there was more to be said
(see, *e.g.*, 32:1, 36ff., dated in Zedekiah's tenth year). For the
kingdom of man, nothing.

---

[73] Rev. 18:21.

EPILOGUE: Jeremiah 52

Jerusalem and Babylon:
A historical footnote

The final sentence of chapter 51 makes it clear that this further chapter is an editor's coda to the book. It is written in fact mostly in the very words of 2 Kings 24:18 – 25:30.

A disastrous king   52:1–11

Zedekiah has met us before, chiefly in chapters 34, 37 – 38, as 'a double-minded man, unstable in all his ways',[1] tragically unfit for his role as Nebuchadrezzar's deputy, set between the hammer of Babylon and the anvil of his own people. Timid though he was, he is held responsible for the downward path he trod: breaking faith first with God (2), then with his overlord (3b) and finally with the slaves whom he liberated and heartlessly took back again (34:8, 16, 21).

Jerusalem demolished, depopulated ana desecrated   52:12–23

The siege and fall of Jerusalem (January 588 to July 587) and the dreadful fate of Zedekiah, as described above in verses 4–11, have

---

[1] *Cf.* Jas. 1:8.

already been recounted in 39:1–7. There, the narrative soon went on to follow the fortunes of Jeremiah and the rump of Judah left behind in the homeland. Here, after describing the demolition of the city and the marshalling of the captives, the record concentrates on the methodical removal of everything of value still left to the temple after its plundering a decade before.[2] At that earlier time Jeremiah had rebuked the optimists who promised a rapid return of those treasures, bidding them pray instead that God would spare the rest of the vessels. He had held out little hope of it (for they were in no mood to pray), but he did predict the vessels' return in God's good time.[3] If the present was a dark moment, there was the promise to hold on to; and the very thoroughness of the operation – depressingly businesslike – was to wear a different aspect one day, when the royal treasurer not only produced these sacred objects but 'counted them out to Sheshbazzar the prince of Judah' in their thousands.[4]

The fate of leading citizens   52:24–27

These verses run parallel with 2 Kings 25:18–21. Seraiah was the grandson of the high priest Hilkiah who had discovered the lost book of the law in Josiah's reign.[5] He was himself the grandfather of Joshua-ben-Jozadak, the high priest at the return from exile.[6] So the family line survived his violent death, and another branch of it would produce the great Ezra, a century hence.[7]

The other priest named here, Zephaniah, seems by his high position to have been the one who had passed on a threat of 'the stocks and collar' to Jeremiah over this very question of the temple vessels a few years earlier.[8] On two subsequent occasions he had been part of a deputation from the king to consult the prophet over the siege of Jerusalem.[9] But Jeremiah's call to surrender had seemed too radical, and now the city's leaders had to pay the price that Babylon put on their refusal.

[2] *Cf.* 2 Ki. 24:13.
[3] Je. 27:18–22.
[4] Ezr. 1:7–11.
[5] 2 Ki. 22:8.
[6] Ezr. 3:2.
[7] Ezr. 7:1–5, *cf.* 1 Ch. 6:3–14.
[8] See 29:24–29 and comment, p. 101f.
[9] 21:1ff.; 37:3ff.

Three successive deportations   *52:28–30*

There are some minor puzzles here over dates, since the seventh and eighteenth years of Nebuchadrezzar appear in 2 Kings as his eighth and nineteenth.[10] But these reflect the two ways of dating the king's reign: either from his actual accession (autumn 605) or, in Babylonian reckoning, from his formal enthronement in the new year (spring 604). This passage used the latter, referring to the years 598/7 (King Jehoiachin's captivity), 587 (Zedekiah's) and thirdly, 582/1. The last of these, not recorded elsewhere, could well belong to the reprisals for Gedaliah's murder, for fear of which a large group fled to Egypt, as described in chapters 42 – 44.

The total of captives in verse 28 is harder to reconcile with 2 Kings. John Bright suggests that 3,023 may have been 'an exact count of adult males', while the figures in 2 Kings 24:14, 16 (10,000 and 8,000) are 'probably round numbers including all the people deported',[11] *i.e.*, taking in the men's families. On verse 29 he comments likewise that the 832 'probably counts only adult males, and possibly only people taken from the urban population of Jerusalem'.[12]

A gleam of light   *52:31–34*

The final words of 2 Kings now close this book as well, surely with the same motive: to show the first faint promise of a better future. But thirty-seven years in prison! And so long a sentence for a reign of three months.[13] Of course his custody was a precaution, since a king in exile is a focus for rebellion; and perhaps this king had briefly shown himself to be too much his father's son.[14] But the disproportion between three months and thirty-seven years highlights the injustice of a system that fails to respect the biblical

[10] 2 Ki. 24:12; 25:8. Je. 52:12 is evidently copied from the latter, but its mention of the tenth day of the month is either a scribal error (frequent with numerals) or possibly reflects the difference between Nebuzaradan's arrival and the start of operations.

[11] Bright, p. 369. Bright rejects an alternative theory (Ewald) that the 'seventh' year (28) should read 'seventeenth', referring to the year before Jerusalem's capitulation and thus to the captives taken from the surrounding country (*cf.* Keil, 2, pp. 328–329; Streane, p. 351).

[12] *A History of Israel* (SCM Press, ³ 1980), p. 330, n. 61.

[13] 2 Ki. 24:8.

[14] This seems implied both in the wording of 2 Ki. 24:1, 9, and in the fact that Nebuchadrezzar decided – mistakenly – to replace him with the pliant Zedekiah (2 Ki. 24:17).

criteria: first, the factual, retrospective proviso, 'If it is true and certain that such ... has been done', and secondly the retributive principle, 'if the guilty man deserves ...' [15] Such criteria of fact and desert set limits to what a Nebuchadrezzar or a Caiaphas may think 'expedient' (Jn. 11:50), and to the social bias of the times (Lv. 19:15).

Happily, Amel-marduk (to give him his native name) was generosity itself, doing everything for the ex-prisoner's need of acceptance, self-respect and security – not content with merely having him released. The extra honour of pre-eminence (32), for the king of so small a people, surely pointed to two things: the wisdom of the peaceable attitude that had been commended in the letter to the captives (29:4–7); and the gracious hand of God in moving the king to show this favour.

So the historical appendix to the book is not the anticlimax that it might have seemed to be. Its tragic record shows the sober truth of Jeremiah's warnings, proving them to be anything but the 'jeremiads' of a pessimist. But the closing paragraph, too, bears out his message, which looked beyond captivity to restoration, of which this royal gesture was a divinely prompted foretaste.

To borrow, in conclusion, better words than mine: 'In its present context the chapter seems to say: the divine word both has been fulfilled – and will be fulfilled!' [16]

[15] Dt. 17:4; 25:2.
[16] Bright, p. 370.

APPENDIX A

Sin, judgment, repentance, grace and salvation in the preaching of Jeremiah

Sin

'Run to and fro', God had said, 'through the streets of Jerusalem...to see if you can find a man, one who does justice and seeks truth; that I may pardon her.'

The result was shattering. From the poor and ignorant to the great and knowledgeable, only hypocrisy, hardness and defiance met the searcher. Was this, as B. Duhm suggested, the country lad's first encounter with the capital – an experience, like Luther's pilgrimage to Rome, that marked him for life? This degree of novelty is hardly possible, since Anathoth was only an hour's walk from Jerusalem; yet Jeremiah's account leaves no doubt of the eye-opening effect of this assignment on him, giving impetus to his search into the depths of the phenomenon.

The acts of sin that he denounces are a familiar list, from idolatry[1]

---

[1] *E.g.*, 2:27–28.

to injustice,[2] from spiritual adultery[3] to physical,[4] and so on. But above all he probes into the state of mind that produces them, revealed as:

Refusal to think

'For my people are foolish, they know me not; they are stupid children, they have no understanding' (4:22). More exactly, they refuse the evidence of their eyes and ears (5:21). Even at the lowest level of religious thought they neither stand in awe of God's power (5:22) –

> Do you not fear me? says the Lord;
> Do you not tremble before me?

– nor appreciate his gifts (5:24–25). In New Testament terms, they have not even the Prodigal's common sense and realism, and they disdain the response which God requires of even the heathen: to 'honour him as God' and 'give thanks to him' (*cf.* Rom. 1:20–21). So it is not a restatement of the truth that they need, for, like the heathen, they suppress it. The very birds are wiser (8:7):

> Even the stork in the heavens
>   knows her times;
> and the turtledove, swallow, and crane
>   keep the time of their coming;
> but my people know not
>   the ordinance of the Lord.

Refusal to listen

As people unconverted they have no ears for God. In the Old Testament terms of 6:10 (see margin), 'Behold, their ears are uncircumcised [*i.e.*, profane, unsurrendered], they cannot listen'. So they have never accepted the correction and commands that cut back human waywardness and train a godly character (7:28):

> This is the nation that did not obey[5] the voice of the Lord

---

[2] *E.g.*, 2:34.
[3] *E.g.*, 3:6–10.
[4] *E.g.*, 5:7–8.
[5] Lit. 'listen to'.

their God, and did not accept discipline; truth has
perished; it is cut off from their lips.

For to be untaught by God is not to remain neutral, poised between
truth and error, between good and evil, but to be steeped in man's
alternative ethos, well versed in what is wrong (4:22):

> They are skilled in doing evil,
> but how to do good they know not.

Infatuation

They are as unbiddable as a creature inflamed with desire: the wild
ass on heat (2:24), or the absconding wife who says, 'It is hopeless,
for I have loved strangers, and after them I will go' (2:25). This
perverse love is the despair of Israel's would-be Rescuer. If there are
false teachers, 'my people love to have it so' (5:31); if there is a
straight path, 'They have loved to wander' (14:10) – not merely like
sheep going astray but 'like a horse plunging headlong into battle'
(8:6). To invitations and warnings alike their response is 'We will
not...We will not...' (6:16–17).

Deep-seated evil

Many metaphors are needed for this. The guilt of this generation is
an indelible stain (2:22), a diamond-cut engraving (17:1). Their
wicked ways are no surface-trickle but an unfailing well (6:7). They
are so used to doing wrong, so trained to it, that it would take a
miracle to change them (13:23):

> Can the Ethiopian change his skin
> or the leopard his spots?
> Then also you can do good
> who are accustomed[6] to do evil.

But most radical of all is the diagnosis of the human heart, not
merely of the contemporary generation, in 17:9:

> The heart is deceitful above all things,
> and desperately corrupt;[7]
> who can understand it?

[6] Or, 'schooled'.
[7] Or, 'desperately sick' (NEB). On this expression, and on 'deceitful', see p. 73.

— for sin makes not only self-cure impossible (*cf.* 30:12–13) but even self-knowledge. Notice that Jeremiah applied these findings not least to himself: see his 'Heal me...' (17:14) and his very necessary openness to correction in his pleas and protests to the one 'who triest the heart and the mind' (11:20; 12:3; 10:23–24). Notice too the relevance of the new covenant (31:31ff.) to the 'heart' as seen here in its guilt (17:1) and depravity (17:9).

Judgment

At least three things are clear in the many sayings on this topic. Judgment, which is retributive (*e.g.* 50:29; 51:56) but potentially corrective (10:24; 30:11), is seen as:

A *moral necessity*

This comes out strongly in chapter 5, with the fruitless search of Jerusalem for a single reason to spare her. The repetition of the word 'pardon' in verses 1 and 7 underlines God's leaning towards mercy; but also, in the end, the transition from an open situation to a closed one: namely, from the bidding,

> Search...that I may pardon her,

to the conclusion, as the picture emerges,

> How can I pardon you?

By expressing this as a question, God spreads his judgment before us as something self-authenticating, having nothing arbitrary to it, nothing even avoidable.

As chapter 5 goes on, unfolding further evidence, it is with a question again, twice over (9, 29), that we are made to contemplate this moral necessity:

> Shall I not punish them for these things?

Jeremiah's exclamation as he searched Jerusalem has already answered for us (3):

> O Lord, do not thy eyes look for truth?

A logical necessity

From this angle, judgment is seen as what the act itself produces ('the fruit of their devices', 6:19) – or, with matters of omission, what overtakes one through neglect. To stay with chapter 5, two sayings put this sufficiently to us; first, in 5:25,

> Your iniquities have turned these [blessings] away,
> and your sins have kept good from you;

and secondly, in a question (again!) addressed to a people who will not face facts,

> How will you fare at the end of it all? (5:31, NEB).

From their own lips, as if in reply, we learn of the situation which anticipates the final state:

> The harvest is past, the summer is ended,
> and we are not saved (8:20, *cf.* 13).

There is no arguing with that. In the words of 2:17 (*cf.* 4:18),

> Have you not brought this upon yourself...?

A controlled operation

Even when an oracle of judgment is in full flow, we are liable to be brought up short by the concession, 'but make not a full end' (5:10).[8] Certainly the present set-up must go, and Jeremiah must not waste time praying for 'this people';[9] yet there will be a remnant brought back from captivity (23:3; 24:4–7; 31:7) to enjoy 'a future and a hope' (29:11). This restraint of judgment is even promised (along with due chastening) to certain of Israel's heathen neighbours;[10] and significantly Jeremiah finds that he himself deserves no softer handling (10:24, *cf.* 30:11b):

> Correct me, O Lord, but in just measure;
> not in thy anger, lest thou bring me to nothing.

---

[8] This is too much for JB, which deletes the word 'not' (!) at 4:27 and 5:10, despite retaining it at 5:18; 30:11, *etc.*

[9] 7:16; 11:14; 14:11, esp. 15:1.

[10] 46:26; 48:47, *etc.*

Repentance

In the Old Testament, repentance is expressed in terms now of the emotions,[11] now of the will.[12] Often both are used together. Jeremiah varies his appeals, somewhat as follows:

Stop and think

'After I was instructed...I was ashamed' (31:19) – for a great enemy of repentance is thoughtlessness, whether as mindless superstition or as absorption with the nearest thing. On the former of these, where no-one notices the difference between God and Baal,

> *Look* at your way in the valley;
> *know* what you have done (2:23).

And on the second, with its frivolity,

> How lightly you gad about,
> changing your way! (2:36)

– changing, that is, only as the fancy takes you, not as you need to change:

> No man repents of his wickedness,
> saying, 'What have I done?' (8:6).

Plead guilty

This does not come easily (3:3):

> ...you have a harlot's brow,
> you refuse to be ashamed.

When God shows displeasure you take no correction (2:30): instead, you take umbrage and complain[13] of his unfairness. Even when caught red-handed, you say, 'I am innocent' (2:34–35).

While this attitude persists, judgment is the only answer (2:35b),

---

[11] *niham*, be sorry, rue, feel compunction.
[12] *šûb*, turn, return.
[13] This word in 2:29a is borrowed from litigation.

however much God may long to heal the breach:

> Return...for I am merciful...
> *Only acknowledge your guilt,*
>> that you rebelled against the Lord your God (3:12–13).

Prove your sincerity

To 'acknowledge your guilt' (see above) and then persist in it, is to sin with your eyes open. 'Behold, you have spoken', says God, referring to the gushing words of 3:4–5a, 'but you have done all the evil that you could' (5b) – and it was this brazen hypocrisy that made 'false Judah' more guilty than 'faithless Israel' (3:11). The 'Den of Robbers' sermon of chapter 7 develops the theme at white heat; but the opening verses of chapter 4 put the matter positively, leading to the appeal of 4:3b–4a (NIV):

> Break up your unploughed ground,
>> and do not sow among thorns.
> Circumcise yourselves to the Lord,
>> circumcise your hearts

– with all that this implies of native hardness humbled, the old habits uprooted, and the carnal outlook renounced for the spiritual.

Come home to God

Without this dimension, repentance would be no more than self-reform. The personal nature of the call is put with emphasis in 4:1a by the order of the words in the second line:

> If you return, O Israel, says the Lord,
>> *to me* you should return.

The whole thrust of the opening chapters reinforces this by their main metaphor of the truant wife and her recall.

But as well as being God*ward*, repentance will have to be God-*given*. In a vision of better days to come we hear a chastened Ephraim confessing this at last, in words of eager simplicity: literally, 'Turn me, that I may turn'.[14] This brings us to the next subject.

---

[14] 31:18b (17b, Heb.).

Grace

The word 'grace', rendering the Hebrew *ḥēn* ('grace' or 'favour'), is found only at 31:2, where God's ancient goodness to a helpless Israel is the model of what he will yet do for them.

> The people who survived the sword
> found grace[15] in the wilderness.

But this divine initiative towards the helpless and undeserving is assumed in all the promises, and its motivation made vivid by familiar analogies. To God, Israel is, for example, a flock which he cannot bear to see ill-shepherded (23:1–4); a patient whom none but he can heal (30:12–13, 17a); a seeming outcast whom people must no longer taunt as 'Zion, for whom no one cares!' (30:17b). On the contrary, they are the work of art he has set his hand to (18:1ff.); the people he is pledged to for ever (33:19ff.); above all, the family whom he loves with everlasting love (31:3). In fact, Israel means to him what every member of a family can mean in turn: the wife whom he must win back (2:2; 3:12); the wayward daughter (31:22a); the rebellious sons who are yet the apple of his eye (3:22; 31:20). Nothing of this is theirs by their deserving.

Salvation

True to the Old Testament's way of speaking, and to Israel's desperate plight at the time, Jeremiah uses the words 'save' and 'deliver' almost invariably in the sense of literal, physical rescue. His vision does not stop there, but first we should see something of what God was saying at this immediate level.

Individually, to Jeremiah's rescuer Ebed-melech (39:18) and to the loyal Baruch (45:5) God pledged the saving of their lives, but

[15] Even here we look in vain for the NT word *charis*, in the LXX of this verse, since that version read the Heb. for 'heat' (*ḥōm*) at this point!

little else, in the coming holocaust at Jerusalem. But in the similar word to Jeremiah,

> I am with you
> to save you and deliver you,[16]

the context promised more than safety: rather, the spiritual stamina to hold out against lifelong persecution. There is also one point, even if only one, at which Jeremiah uses the word 'save' to pray for personal, inward renewal:

> Heal me, O Lord, and I shall be healed;
> save me, and I shall be saved;
> for thou art my praise (17:14).

At the national level, however, the early chapters are overhung with the threat of judgment in the form of military invasion, from which it becomes increasingly clear that nothing can now save this people: neither their last-resort prayer to the Lord ('Arise and save us!' 2:27) nor the gods which they cling on to ('Let *them* arise, if they can save you', 2:28). God's appeals for a repentance that would avert the national disaster,

> O Jerusalem, wash your heart from wickedness,
> that you may be saved (4:14),

give way to his commands to Jeremiah against praying 'for this people' – *i.e.*, for captivity to be averted[17] – and to the conclusion,

> The harvest is past, the summer is ended,
> and we are not saved (8:20).

But looking at last beyond the judgment, salvation becomes the leading theme of the later chapters, especially 30 – 33:

> for lo, I will save you from afar,
> and your offspring from the land of their captivity.
> Jacob shall return and have quiet and ease,
> and none shall make him afraid.
> For I am with you to save you, says the Lord (30:10–11).

It is presented first and foremost as a restoring of their fortunes,[18] to

---

[16] 15:20, *cf.* 1:19.
[17] *Cf.* 7:16; 15:1–2.
[18] This expression (see on 33:6, p. 114) comes seven times in chs. 30 – `3

'rebuild them as they were at first' (33:7). This is painted in glowing colours as the enjoyment again of their peace with God (33:8), their long-lost unity (32:39), their land (31:8), their city (30:18; 31:38–40), temple (33:11), king (the ideal 'David', 30:9; 33:15), priests (33:18ff.), festivals (33:10–11), offerings (33:18) and sociable delights (30:19; 31:4, 13; 33:11).

A modest foretaste of these things was in store for them at the Exile's end; but the promise of 'a righteous Branch...for David', ruling over a 'saved' (*i.e.*, secure) Judah and a Jerusalem which would reflect the righteousness of Yahweh (33:14–16), transports us into the messianic age; nothing less. With this clue we must see the details that we have just looked at, not in their imperfect, post-exilic state alone, but as the Messiah would fulfil them – church, priesthood, temple, sacrifices, and all. Here are the Old Testament's separate strands of salvation, which Christ would weave together in the perfection of his person and work.

While we see this fulfilment now with the privilege of hindsight, there were already indications in the book, in plain language, that God was planning a more radical work than that of restoring Israel's outward fortunes. In a remarkable passage, 3:15–18, he had foretold the day when the very ark of the covenant would be obsolete, 'not...remembered, or missed'; but even this is outstripped in the famous prophecy of 31:31ff. which looks forward to the replacing of the old covenant itself by the new, with the gift of heart-obedience, personal relationship with God, and full atonement.

This, in the terms of 1 Peter 1:10ff., is the 'salvation' into which the prophets 'searched and inquired', greeting it from afar, as 'the Spirit of Christ within them' spoke of the blessings which we now enjoy.

In the words of John Skinner, this prophecy 'threw a bright beam of light across the ages; and it falls at last on One who is the Yea and the Amen to all the promises of God – on Jesus the Mediator of the New Covenant, and the Author of eternal salvation'.[19]

[19] Skinner, p.334.

APPENDIX B

The chapters of the book in their chronological setting

The prologue and part one: chapters 1 – 20

These chapters, for the most part, probably cover the period 627–605 BC, *i.e.*, from the thirteenth year of Josiah (1:2; 3:6) to the fourth year of Jehoiakim (25:1, 3). The prophet regarded the year 605 as ending his first long period of preaching ('for twenty-three years': see 25:1, 3); and he was instructed to collect these oracles into a single scroll (36:1–2).

Since the next chapters, 21 – 45, are mostly given dates, all of which (with the possible exception of 26:1) belong to the final twenty years of Jeremiah's ministry (605–*c*.585), it seems reasonable to view chapters 1 – 20 as preserving substantially the contents of the scroll read to King Jehoiakim in 604, the year after its compiling.

Apart from the year mentioned in 1:2, however, and the allusion to 'the days of King Josiah' in 3:6, no individual dates are given in these twenty chapters, and few are deducible – with the possible exception of the following:

   a. Chapter 7, *if* it is a longer account of the sermon preached in chapter 26 'In the beginning of the reign of Jehoiakim' (26:1);

b. Chapters 11 and 12. See the comments there, arguing for a close connection with the finding of the law-book in 622/1;

c. Chapter 13 (or part of it), since verse 18 is evidently addressing King Jehoiachin and his mother Nehushta, who were exiled in 597;

d. Chapters 18 – 20, since they culminate in Jeremiah's ordeal in the pillory, suggesting that the regime is no longer that of King Josiah; therefore post-609.

We should be warned, however, against constructing a chronology of this section: first by the presence of point *c*, above (already addressing these two people by their royal titles, therefore presumably spoken not before 598/7); and secondly by the analogy of the dated chapters in Part Two, which disregard the dictates of time in their arrangement, as the following table shows.

Part two: chapters 21 – 45 (mostly 605–*c.*585)

For the time-shifts in these carefully dated oracles, see the opening remarks on these chapters, p. 83.

Chapters	Events or Subjects	Years
21	The final siege of Jerusalem begins	588
22	Oracles on kings, from Josiah to (Je)coniah	598
23	False shepherds; righteous Branch; false prophets	No date
24	Good figs and bad	597 or after
25	Seventy-years' exile predicted	605
26	The 'Shiloh' sermon	609 or after
27 – 28	The call to accept the yoke of Babylon	594
29	The letter to the captives	After 597
30 – 31	The 'book of hope'	No date
32 – 33	Jeremiah buys property while in prison, as a sign	588/7

34	Temporary lifting of the siege; exploiting of slaves	588
35	A lesson from the Rechabites	After 601[1]
36	The scroll and its burning	605–604
37	Jeremiah arrested and imprisoned	588
38	The miry pit	588/7
39	The city falls	587
40	Jeremiah joins Gedaliah at Mizpah	587
41	Gedaliah assassinated	587 or after
42 – 43	The emigration to Egypt, taking Jeremiah	587 or after
44	The émigrés defend their apostasy	c. 585?
45	An early message to Baruch	605

Part three: chapters 46 – 51: Oracles on the nations

These are undated; evidently uttered at various times and circulated separately before being brought together to form a section on their own in the completed book. In the Septuagint (LXX) version they are not only in a quite different sequence, but are found (appropriately enough) between verses 13a and 15 of our chapter 25.

Epilogue: chapter 52

This historical footnote was added after King Jehoiachin's release in 561; indeed after his subsequent death, of which the date is unknown.

[1] Cf. 35:11 with 2 Ki. 24:1–2.

APPENDIX C

A table of dates

Years	Events or Subjects	
640/39	Josiah becomes king, aged eight	2 Ch. 34:1
628	Josiah begins his reforms	2 Ch. 34:3
627	Jeremiah begins his ministry	Je. 1:2; 25:3
626	Nabopolassar founds the neo-Babylonian empire	
622/1	The book of the law discovered	2 Ch. 34:8, 14
612	The fall of Nineveh, capital of Assyria	Cf. Na. 1:1ff.
609	Josiah killed in battle	2 Ch. 35:20–25
	Jehoahaz king for three months	2 Ch. 36:1–3
	Jehoiakim made king by Pharaoh Neco	2 Ch. 36:4
605	Nebuchadrezzar routs Egyptians at Carchemish	Je. 46:2
	Daniel and a select few deported to Babylon	Dn. 1:1–7[1]
604	Jeremiah's scroll read out to Jehoiakim and burnt	Je. 36
601	Jehoiakim rebels against Babylon	2 Ki. 24:1
598	Jehoiakim is deposed, and dies	2 Ch. 36:6
597	The first main captivity. Jeconiah (Jehoiachin) and the skilled men and the temple treasures deported	2 Ki. 24:12–16
	Zedekiah made king	2 Ki. 24:17
593	Zedekiah summoned to Babylon	Je. 51:59
588	Zedekiah, for treachery, is besieged in Jerusalem	Je. 52:3–4
587	Fall of Jerusalem. Second stage of captivity	Je. 39
587 and after	Gedaliah appointed governor. Joined by Jeremiah	Je. 40:5–6
	Gedaliah assassinated by Ishmael	Je. 41:2
	Refugees flee to Egypt, taking Jeremiah with them	Je. 42 – 43
582/1	A third deportation to Babylon	Je. 52:30
561	Jehoiachin released from prison	Je. 52:31–34
539	Fall of Babylon	Dn. 5:30
539/8	Cyrus the Persian liberates the captives	Ezr. 1:1–4

[1] Jehoiakim's 'third year' (Dn. 1:1) reflects the Babylonian numbering of a king's years not from his accession but from his subsequent enthronement. See on 52:28–30.